**W9-BXR-233**

LIVINGSTON PUBLIC LIBRARY
10 Robert H. Harp Drive
Livingston, NJ 07039

# BIG IN CHINA

## MY UNLIKELY ADVENTURES RAISING A FAMILY, PLAYING THE BLUES, AND BECOMING A STAR IN BEIJING

# Alan Paul

HARPER

*An Imprint of* HarperCollins*Publishers*

www.harpercollins.com

BIOG
PAUL

BIG IN CHINA. Copyright © 2011 by Alan Paul. All rights reserved. Printed in the United States of America. No part of this book may be used or reproduced in any manner whatsoever without written permission except in the case of brief quotations embodied in critical articles and reviews. For information, address HarperCollins Publishers, 10 East 53rd Street, New York, NY 10022.

HarperCollins books may be purchased for educational, business, or sales promotional use. For information, please write: Special Markets Department, HarperCollins Publishers, 10 East 53rd Street, New York, NY 10022.

"You're Gonna Make Me Lonesome When You Go" by Bob Dylan.
Copyright © 1974 by Ram's Horn Music; renewed 2002 by Ram's Horn Music. All rights reserved. International copyright secured. Reprinted by permission.

"Hold On To What You Got" by Johnny Copeland.
Copyright © JoClyde Music All rights reserved. Reprinted by permission.

FIRST EDITION

Designed by Renato Stanisic

Library of Congress Cataloging-in-Publication Data has been applied for.

ISBN 978-0-06-199315-2

11 12 13 14 15  OV/RRD  10 9 8 7 6 5 4 3 2 1

3-2-11 HL

TO BECKY

# AUTHOR'S NOTE

Some conversations and events have been condensed, but all quotes and names are real, with the exception of Yechen. This was my Chinese teacher's nickname, and how he asked to be identified.

The RMB-to-dollar exchange rate varied from roughly 8:1 when we arrived in Beijing to about 6.7:1 when we departed. I used 7:1 throughout the book.

I used China's standard pinyin romanization method of spelling.

# CONTENTS

# PROLOGUE

**X**IAMEN, CHINA—I stood in the spotlight at the center of the broad stage, feeling exposed and alone. My bandmates, who were usually by my side, were several steps behind, leaving the eyes of five thousand Chinese people solely upon me. They were ready to be wowed.

My band, Woodie Alan, was headlining the Xiamen Beach Festival, a big deal in this beautiful southern China port city. The MC had just announced us, in Mandarin, to the sprawling crowd as "Beijing's best band." It was a title we had earned in a magazine readers' poll a few months earlier and that we were now confronted with validating.

Smoke and bubble machines surrounded us, along with a five-camera TV crew who was filming the performance for broadcast throughout Fujian Province, home to forty-four million people. A kneeling cameraman pointed his lens at my face, which was illuminated by a blinding bank of spotlights. I blinked into the glare and felt my legs wobble and my throat grow tight.

I stepped to the mic, apologized for my bad Chinese, and gave a short, rambling thank-you: "I am American. My friends are Chinese. Together, we are one band. We believe that with music, there is one people; no Americans, no Chinese, no Xiameners or Beijingers; just people."

I knew it was a cheap trick—Chinese people love hearing foreigners speak their language—but I wanted to make the effort to reach out, and I truly believed the sentiments, even if I could only express them in a string of half-formed clichés.

The loud cheer calmed me as the rhythm section kicked off a hard-driving beat. I shut my eyes and laid into the haunting, slinky opening riff of "Beijing Blues," one of the first songs I ever wrote and now our signature tune. The crowd responded, though most of them could not understand a word I was singing—something that always gave me a proud sense of transcending language with emotion and music.

Fifty minutes and eight songs later we walked off to applause and met on the side of the stage, exchanging hugs and handshakes, and then sharing a warm Tsingtao beer. I poured from one large green bottle into four tiny plastic cups, which we hoisted together in a toast to our success.

It was a scene I never could have envisioned three years earlier, when my wife and I walked off a plane in Beijing with three little kids in tow. I didn't speak a word of Chinese, knew little about the country or the expatriate life I was embarking upon, and had never been in a real band despite years of playing guitar. Now here I was fronting a band with three fantastic Chinese musicians as the headline act of this festival.

Following our impromptu backstage celebration, my lone American bandmate, Dave Loevinger, and I rejoined our families, who had proudly watched our performance from the front row. Fans surrounded us asking for autographs and wanting to pose for pictures together. A giant festival poster we had autographed earlier that day loomed behind us.

"File this under, 'Never thought it would happen,' " said Dave. We were standing next to a smiling woman holding her fingers up in a V, the sign virtually every Chinese person flashes when being photographed.

Over the next few days on our continuing tour of south-central China, we would do four radio interviews, perform live on the air on the largest station in Hunan Province, sign life-sized posters, and have drunken Chinese mobsters insist on sharing their cognac and Cuban cigars as thanks for our music.

I smiled for the picture, then turned to look out over the exiting crowd on the moonlit beach, the Taiwan Straits stretching behind the stage. Waves crashed onto the shore where Chinese lanterns had gently floated out to sea earlier that evening in a celebration of the fall festival.

I took it all in and wondered just how I had gotten here.

# CHAPTER 1

# COME TO THE EDGE

Three years earlier, I'd looked at my wife, Rebecca, through feverish eyes, cold sweat plastered over my forehead, and told her that I wasn't quite ready to sign on the dotted line. I couldn't agree to pack up our three kids, abandon life in idyllic, leafy Maplewood, New Jersey, and move to Beijing. Not just now.

I shifted in my sweat-soaked coach-class seat and put down the book I couldn't focus on anyhow. I struggled to explain why I was hesitating. "I'm not sure this whole thing is such a good idea. I need more time to think."

We were thirty-five thousand feet up, in the middle of a fourteen-hour flight back to the United States from a weeklong "look-see visit" to Beijing, undertaken to decide whether Rebecca would accept the job as the *Wall Street Journal*'s China bureau chief. I had pushed her to explore this opportunity and I was extremely enthusiastic about it all week, loving everything about China: the energy, the culture, the sites, and the food. Even the pea-soup pollution didn't give me second thoughts. Within two days we were both ready for her to accept the job.

We started taking pictures to show our three kids: Jacob, seven; Eli, four; and Anna, twenty-one months. We wanted China to look like a fun, inviting place rather than a scary, exotic destination so we visited parks, playgrounds, their future school, our house-to-be, and perhaps the world's largest ball pit at the wonderfully named Fundazzle play space.

Now I was having second thoughts, my wavering triggered by the very thing that had fueled my fervor: food. I had eaten my way through Beijing, throwing caution to the wind once I realized just how different—and how much better—the cuisine in Beijing was compared with any other Chinese food I had ever tried. I wolfed down bowls of wide handmade noodles, meat pancakes, dozens of dumplings, crispy Peking duck, fiery Sichuan beef sliced thin and dunked in a table-side bowl of scorching oil, and huge, earthy wild mushrooms sautéed with giant heads of garlic and hot peppers. I loved it all—until it caught up with me.

I spent my last two days in China mostly lying on my hotel bed, running back and forth to the bathroom and dispatching Rebecca to scrounge for Imodium. My diet was reduced to dry toast and tea.

I didn't feel much better on the long march home. I was drenched in sweat, clutching my armrests and sucking down sodas as fast as the flight attendant could bring them. Moving to Beijing suddenly seemed like a very stupid idea.

"Don't commit to anything," I said, staggering weak-legged off the plane. "What are we getting ourselves into?"


I WAS PUTTING Rebecca in a bad spot. She had accepted the job in Beijing and begun working out details. My enthusiasm had gotten her to raise her hand for the job; it had driven our whirlwind week touring Beijing; and it had allowed her to start imagining herself in the position.

Now I was hedging and she was understandably confused. It seemed like all this fuss was over an upset stomach, but it was deeper than that. The illness had shaken me, causing me to truly doubt the wisdom of moving.

We had a house we liked in a neighborhood that we loved. Maplewood, New Jersey, is a tree-lined town of colonial homes, filled with a diverse mix of families. Just a half-hour train ride from Manhattan, it is an island of peace and calm, with chirping birds and a friendly, interesting population that belies most suburban stereotypes. Writing contracts with *Guitar World* and *Slam* magazines provided a flexible freelance lifestyle backed by the stability of steady money, allowing me to make a living writing about two of my passions, music and basketball.

Most importantly, moving would mean cutting the cord on a fantastic network—a pair of aunts and uncles on the block, my sister and her family ten minutes away, and two sets of parents who visited often and with whom we were very close. We often called our family cluster "the commune" or "shtetl," evoking the European Jewish ghettos where our ancestors lived. This old-fashioned way of life suited us beautifully.

Our support system permitted us to maintain our balance and allowed Rebecca to work long hours without me growing resentful or feeling isolated. I had previously discouraged her from pursuing *Journal* jobs in San Francisco, Chicago, and Washington, D.C., because moving just seemed too risky. Yet neither of us was ready to acknowledge that this was where we would spend the rest of our lives. It was impossible to imagine moving, and equally far-fetched to contemplate spending the next thirty years in the same house. It felt like we had at least one great adventure in us.

Scratching that itch with an overseas posting had simply never occurred to us. Rebecca had not even told me about the China opening, assuming I would refuse to make such a move with three young kids. I heard her casually mention it to a friend, who had asked about the scope of the *Journal*'s operations over lunch.

"The paper has bureaus all over the world," Rebecca said. "They just posted the China bureau chief job in Beijing."

"Beijing?" I perked up, tuning into the conversation from the pizza I was eating with my kids at an adjoining table. "Are you applying for that?"

She was shocked. Though even I didn't fully understand my reflexive reaction, I had a nagging "now or never" sensation as soon as I heard about this opportunity; a move out of the country was only going to get harder as our children got older. And my desire to remain in Maplewood long term actually made moving to China more appealing because a foreign posting was understood to be for a limited time, unlike a more definitive domestic move. We could even keep our house, allowing us to maintain a solid safety net.

I never wavered from the first moment I heard about the opening—until that illness knocked the confidence out of me. As I sulked, a rare silence set in between Rebecca and me. Friends and family who had enjoyed my enthusiastic, passionate e-mails about the great Chinese food now teased me about getting sick. I did not admit my new hesitations to anyone else as I began to work through them.

Maybe I had been viewing the whole thing backward by focusing on how much my career would suffer in a move. Beijing could well open more doors than it closed. During our visit, I had hatched a vague idea about writing a column about my expat life and put together an imprecise, but inspired, pitch. When the editor of the *Wall Street Journal Online* quickly showed interest, I was reminded that there were a lot of opportunities hidden amid the uncertainties.

I had to acknowledge the uncomfortable truth that I was growing restless, stuck in a velvet-lined rut. I was finally starting to feel a simmering resentment toward Rebecca's career, which was thriving while mine meandered. I worried about this festering problem after a long, easy relationship based around supporting each other's work while carving out very different niches.

I had never really followed a career plan, trusting that something new and exciting would come up. This worked for years, but I was now in a long stretch of promising ideas leading only to dead ends. The future no longer seemed limitless as I approached my fortieth birthday. A new *Guitar World* owner wanted me to start coming into the office every day, threatening my routine. Our whole family structure would crumble if I also began commuting into New York. I had happily assumed primary child-care duties when Jacob was born, but managing three kids' schedules was increasingly complex.

I thought about a conversation I had with my father a few months earlier, just after the Beijing job had presented itself. We were riding up a Colorado chairlift on a blustery day, and he wondered why we were hesitating at all. I was born in Anchorage, Alaska, toward the end of a three-year adventure my parents took over their own families' objections. This was one of the best decisions they had ever made, he said.

"It still defines us in some ways forty years later, and you'll probably end up saying the same thing," he said. "It seems to me that you can't say no to this."

I had embraced those words then and I came back to them now.

*You can't say no to this.*

Rebecca had come around to this way of thinking under my prodding. Now it was her turn to push me, by reminding me of my own growing restlessness in suburbia. "We can spend the next three years in China," she said. "Or we can spend them talking about kitchen renovation."

# CHAPTER 2

# THAT'S WHAT LOVE WILL MAKE YOU DO

Rebecca—Becky to me—and I met at the *Michigan Daily*, the University of Michigan's student newspaper. I watched her rise to the top of that intensely political, balkanized organization while creating virtually no enemies.

After graduation, we traveled to Florida in search of jobs, each interviewing at six newspapers. She got five offers, while I received a half of one—for a part-time position at the smallest place we visited.

Becky's intelligence and composure were obvious. What really made her different was that burning ambition did not prevent her from being ready to put her shoulder to the wheel of any job, no doubt a testament to her roots in blue-collar Bay City, Michigan.

I, on the other hand, radiated ambivalence. My passion lay in music writing, and I had already had some freelance success, even interviewing Eric Clapton. After that, it was hard to feign great enthusiasm about covering small-town school board meetings, but I needed a job. I eventually turned down a part-time position in metro New York to move to Tampa Bay with Rebecca, following my instincts and believing that if I trusted in the relationship, good things would happen.

I wrote a series of music stories for small magazines and hooked on as a stringer for the *St. Petersburg Times*. I was honing my craft but after earning $8,000 my first year and despairing of ever moving beyond Ramen noodle wages, I applied to graduate school, intent on becoming a teacher. Then I was offered a job as managing editor at *Guitar World*, which a new editor ambitiously planned to turn into the leading musician's magazine. It felt like winning the lottery. I started work in New York while Becky began looking for a new job that would allow her to join me.

She was following our unspoken agreement that we would each pursue job opportunities and move for each other as necessary. This subtly shifted over the years as her career at the *Wall Street Journal* thrived and I settled in as a freelancer. Ten years before the China move, we had relocated from Manhattan to Ann Arbor, Michigan, when Rebecca was hired by the *Journal*'s Detroit bureau. I became *Guitar World*'s online editor and senior writer and soon was also writing for a host of publications, from *Slam* to the *New Yorker*.

I had landed in a better place after sacrificing for Rebecca's career. Seventeen years into our relationship, it once again felt like time to shut my eyes and make a leap of faith.

WE HAD NOT said a word about China to our children. We wanted to wait until we were certain. Then we called a family meeting, sitting together in a circle on our front lawn. Becky and I had rehearsed our pitch, wanting to make sure that they saw it as a grand family adventure.

We showed them the pictures we had carefully taken for exactly this purpose, focusing on seven-year-old Jacob; the other two would surely follow his lead. We began with the photos of Fundazzle's monstrous ball pit.

"I want to go to China!" he exclaimed.

The kids were in.

To HELP ANCHOR my own work life, I wanted to maintain my associations with *Slam* and *Guitar World*, because it scared me to have nothing. The *Slam* editors were interested in occasional reports on Chinese players and even agreed to write a letter opening a Beijing bureau, with me as its chief, which would establish me as a legally credentialed journalist in China.

*Guitar World* was equally accommodating. Over lunch, editor Brad Tolinski said he was happy to continue our working relationship, which had already spanned fifteen years.

"You can keep working for us as long as you're willing to make the time difference your burden and not anyone else's," Brad said, over a cheeseburger at a diner near the magazine's office. "And as long as you still want to work for us."

"What do you mean?"

"I have a feeling you'll find a world of opportunity over there," he said. "You could be the guy who brings the Allman Brothers to the Great Wall. Who knows what you might end up doing?"

A FEW MONTHS after that nerve-racking flight home, Becky and I were headed back to Beijing, with Jacob, Eli, and Anna buckled in beside us.

I had anticipated that boarding a plane to China with

one-way tickets would engender panic, but I felt only relief. Whatever difficulties the transition posed would pale in comparison to the painstaking process of emptying our house and putting our lives in Maplewood on ice.

That had proven to be surprisingly exhausting, like an archaeological dig that became geometrically more difficult as it neared completion. We had sorted our entire house, crammed full from seven years of pack-rat existence, into various piles. We threw away and donated mounds of goods, filled a crate for storage, selected the precious goods we wanted sent in an air shipment that would arrive in two weeks and slapped "sea shipment" stickers on everything else we wanted to move. That would all be loaded onto a sixty-foot container on our little dead-end street and board a literal slow boat to China, arriving two months later.

We also had to clean and prep the house for tenants, and we made it all more difficult by spending two weeks driving around the country on a farewell tour of family and friends. Bending under the stress, I gained ten pounds and resorted to sleeping pills for the first time in my life.

By the day before we left, we were all coming undone. We had moved in across the street with my remarkably accommodating aunt Joan and uncle Ben, dragging everything we were taking to China in a half-dozen "body bag" duffels I bought at an army/navy store. When Ben suggested they might be too big to meet airline regulations, I visited Continental's website and realized that we were indeed way over the size limit. That led to a frenzied shopping trip to Target and a complete repacking.

That evening, Joan walked into her house, looked around at her living room, so covered with our belongings that it looked like a tractor trailer had exploded, and burst out laughing. I appreciated her good humor and tried to share it, but we were beyond frazzled. All this stuff that once seemed crucial now looked like a random, schizoid collection: six pounds of Peet's coffee and a French press; a pharmacy's worth of Motrin, Tylenol, Imodium, shampoo, and contact lens solution; a collection of dolls and stuffed animals; board games; DVDs; clothes; photo albums. It seemed demented to drag so much stuff to China, but this was no time for second thoughts. We shoved everything into the twelve new bags.

It was exhilarating to have all that behind us. The plane was like a meditation chamber where no one could reach us, and we finally had some time to gather our thoughts. I didn't even allow the flight attendant's chiding for having too many things for the children to bother me.

We somehow survived the fourteen-hour flight, much of it spent trying to get Anna to sleep. As the plane finally approached Beijing, I looked out the window at the jagged brown mountains and did a double take; the Great Wall was clearly visible, snaking across the top of the imposing ridges. Sitting by the window with Anna, I excitedly called the boys over. All four of us pressed our faces against the windows.

"Yep," Jacob said. "That's China all right."

For the rest of the descent, Anna continually pointed out the window and said, "That China."

# CHAPTER 3

# ACROSS THE GREAT DIVIDE

Our strangest initial adjustment was getting used to Beijing Riviera, the walled compound where the *Journal* owned a house. It was the kind of place where we would never have chosen to reside in the United States, with manicured streets and houses that looked so similar that Rebecca and I both repeatedly got lost trying to find our home in the first days.

The Singaporean-owned Riviera has more than four hundred large homes painted in muted pastel peaches and yellows. They were all loaded with patios and roof decks that may have made sense in Singapore but were nonsensical in Beijing's harsh winters and dusty, polluted summers. The interiors featured a marble-infused grandiosity, as if Chinese architects had watched soap operas to determine what Western homes should look like. The compound had an overriding country club feel, with a large clubhouse, a gym, and indoor and outdoor pools.

The whole place was hidden from the outside world by cement walls patrolled by a platoon of guards clad in crisp, military-style uniforms. They looked intimidating until you realized that they were just kids, fresh-faced teens newly arrived from China's hinterlands, many sprouting their first tentative mustaches. They all seemed almost scared of us.

Though well inside Beijing's huge municipal borders, Riviera was ten miles from the central city, twice as close as Maplewood is from downtown Manhattan. But our neighborhood was no Maplewood. The city was actually more readily available—you could get anywhere downtown for a $10 cab ride. But it felt far more remote, because the countryside began just outside the compound walls. I enjoyed riding my new bike down rutted half-dirt roads, past greenhouses surrounded by plywood shanties where migrant workers streaming toward Beijing from rural provinces lived, tending vegetable gardens on minuscule plots; no area was too small to hold a plant or vine. Toddlers waddled through it all with their bare bottoms exposed through pants split in two—no need for diapers when you can go anywhere without even pulling down your pants.

Spending so much time on my bike took me back to a far simpler time in life: my Pittsburgh childhood. I recalled a similar thrill of exploration and sense of open-ended possibility during days spent cruising the neighborhood looking for baseball games, trees to climb, or friends to run through backyards with.

It was jolting to travel through rural China and then ride back through the gates into Riviera's serene, Stepford-like calm. The compound was simultaneously a non-Chinese bubble and a paradigm of Chinese living, with the guards and street maids who kept the sidewalks and gutters clean with archaic twig brooms. There was a constant buzz of motorized tricycles delivering groceries and giant water bottles to homes as well as the supplies that fueled endless construction as one home after another was gutted and redone.

Hundreds of day laborers lined up outside the walls to be

signed in every day at 9:00 a.m. Late in the afternoon, they filed out of the compound, covered in grime, walking shoulder to shoulder under the guards' vigilant eyes.

The very existence of places like the Riv was news to me before we made that look-see visit. I had assumed we would be living in a small apartment in the city center, but we ended up with a house that was larger than our place in New Jersey. Riviera was almost ten years old when we arrived, one of the oldest such compounds.

We lived in an area heavy with these places, and Beijing Riviera was a typical name, joined by Capital Paradise, Lemon Lake, River Garden, Legend Garden, Yosemite—pronounced Yo-Sum-Ite by the Europeans—Chateau Regalia, Dynasty Garden, and the immortal Merlin Champagne Town. The large international schools were all nearby, and the compounds still catered largely to expats, though more and more wealthy Chinese were also moving in. The newer developments tended to have even larger, fancier houses, including some with indoor pools.

Many of these places were located a few miles north of us off the busy Jing Shun Lu (Road), a dusty, bustling road where you were equally likely to encounter speeding Audis with blackened windows, shepherds herding flocks of tattered sheep, or mule-drawn wagons weighed down with bricks. Traversing that made arriving at the newer, fancier compounds feel like landing on a moon colony, distant, isolated outposts of a foreign culture.

All these compounds provided a strange, hermetic environment where you might hear a dozen languages being spoken but could get along just fine with English. Our newly arrived kids didn't notice any of this; they seemed to feel like they were on a Florida vacation, with a pool to splash in and countless kids to play with.

The *Journal*'s deputy bureau chief, Kathy Chen, was like our guardian angel, even having stocked our kitchen with milk, juice, Diet Coke, and a $12 box of Cinnamon Toast Crunch. An American-born Chinese who had spent fifteen of the past twenty years in greater China, Kathy had a deep understanding of both the country and the expat scene. She patiently answered our endless questions and steered us through daily life. Just as importantly, our kids were almost identically aged and they immediately became close friends.

Living in a service apartment while our house was being repaired, we did not have a washer or dryer so I dropped our dirty clothes off at the clubhouse laundry service. I was confused when I picked it up the next day and was charged almost $50. When I got home, I realized that everything had been dry-cleaned instead of laundered. The sight of my kids' tiny tighty whities, T-shirts, and sports shorts hanging stiffly starched on hangers, tags stapled on the labels, made me laugh out loud.

The idea of moving my family to China, which seemed so radical back in New Jersey, now appeared to be anything but. I stood around the compound playgrounds, watching a veritable United Nations of children playing together. Our most exotic traits were our gender reversal—my wife was off working while I was patrolling the swings with a host of mothers and Chinese *ayi*s (nannies)—and the mere fact that we were such expat rookies. "Where was your previous posting?" was a common opening question upon meeting someone. I usually answered with one word: "Jersey."

We felt a great sense of relief when our picky little Jacob put on his new uniform for the British Dulwich College of Beijing with no complaints. He had often refused to wear anything that didn't feel exactly right, and all our anxiety about moving to China had been channeled into the looming need to dictate his clothing. We knew we were going to be okay when he got dressed without a hitch; seeing him and Eli run on to the luxurious coach that served as their school bus on the first day without looking back brought tears to Becky's eyes.

Alone every morning, as Rebecca immersed herself in a demanding, intimidating new position and the kids headed to school, I quickly realized that I needed to stay on the move. I started making exploratory rides around the area on my new mountain bike, often ending up at a nearby Starbucks, which I turned into my office, checking e-mail and writing blog posts. I embraced my new anonymity, feeling that it represented a profound opportunity to hit the reboot button on my life.

It felt like we had stepped through a looking glass or fallen through a rabbit hole and emerged in a parallel universe on the other side of the world. With my wife and kids occupied and everybody else I knew sixty-eight hundred miles away, I was free to explore. It felt like I was winking at life and getting away with something. I was energized by the raw thrill of being enmeshed in two new worlds: Beijing and Expat Land.

I met an eight-year-old girl whose mother was Indian and father Dutch but who had never lived anywhere but Beijing. Eli became good friends with a five-year-old British girl with a perfect English accent who was born and raised in Hong Kong. At one school assembly, the principal asked how many kids spoke four languages and about 20 percent raised their hands. All this would soon seem normal, but it amazed me in those early days. Back home, I was a pretty worldly guy; now I felt like I had just fallen off the turnip truck. It took me most of the year to quit assuming that every five-year-old with a proper British accent knew more than me.

I also quickly learned that in Expat Land I was a "trailing spouse," a term I found demeaning for anyone and downright emasculating for a man. This wasn't all new to me. I had not set foot in an office for a decade, and as our kids' primary caregiver I was used to being the only adult male in a room, having chaperoned field trips, helped kindergartners cut and paste, and been surrounded by mothers at countless midday assemblies.

But the dividing line was much sharper in Expat Land. We had uprooted our family and moved to the other side of the world for someone's job, and it was not mine. I also had a certain cool cachet back home, as the guy who wrote about music and basketball and didn't have to shave. Now I was just the dad without a job.

Fellow expats were not the only ones unsure what to make of me. The company driver, Mr. Dou, had to get used not only to having a lady boss, but also to having a male *tai tai* (lady of the house). Like most people in his position, Mr. Dou was at first an intimidating presence, a former military man who was as much a fixer as a driver. He was loyal, efficient, and well skilled in manipulating the Chinese bureaucracy. It felt good to have him on our side.

He picked us up at the airport on day one, and we spent a lot of time together during our first weeks as he ferried us around on the bureaucratic errands necessary for setting up a life—processing visas, getting press credentials, applying for driver's licenses.

One day he took me alone to the massive police station in central Beijing where visas were issued for foreigners and Chinese alike. We were there to secure long-term visas for my kids and me. My journalist credentials as *Slam*'s first Beijing bureau chief had been received from the Ministry of Foreign Affairs and were attached to my application.

This was my first visit to the office, and the long lines of people waiting behind rows of deskbound, uniformed officers intimidated me. Mr. Dou walked directly to the front of the line and dropped our papers in front of an officious-looking cop, but no one objected. The officer took the papers, began reading through them, and marked every other page with a chop, the ink stamps without which nothing is official in China. Suddenly, he stopped chopping and looked up at me. I braced myself, wondering what the problem was.

He smiled and said, in halting English "I very like *Slam*."

As a *Slam* senior writer for a decade. I knew that the magazine had die-hard readers who considered it a basketball bible. But I did not realize how far its reach extended. I thanked him, and he asked, "Who do you think is best Chinese basketball player, after Yao Ming?"

I had no idea, so I told a partial truth: "That's what I'm here to find out."

Mr. Dou watched us with the shocked expression of someone listening to cats chatting. After he and the officer had an animated discussion, Mr. Dou looked at me and chuckled. Something had changed in the way he regarded me. I had earned some face.

I was happy to gain stature in Mr. Dou's eyes, but I was having too much fun to care much what anyone thought. For the past ten years I had juggled assignments for *Slam* and *Guitar World* with domestic responsibilities. Liberated from deadlines and with no immediate economic need to hustle for work, I poured myself into my new blog. I initially viewed it as merely a means of keeping in touch with friends and family, but I quickly realized that keeping this public journal—posting photos and tales about our new life—was transforming me, reigniting my passion for writing.

I began to treat the blog as a job, compelled to make daily

postings. Writing so much for no money represented the economic emancipation that expat living offered, thanks to subsidized housing in a place where everything else cost radically less.

Back in the United States, it felt like we were on a treadmill, struggling to bring in as much as we spent, even as our salaries rose. Now I was free to follow my muse, writing thousands of words a day just to tell the story I wanted to tell.

Just before graduating from college, I self-published a book of satirical columns I had written for the *Michigan Daily* under the pseudonym Fat Al. In a short introduction, I wrote, "If you can't do it with passion, don't do it." I had tried to continue living by that creed, but it had become an ever-harder standard to maintain. Now, it suddenly seemed attainable again.

Some people reading my blog back home noticed the changes.

"Something is happening to you, Alan," my aunt Carrie Wells e-mailed from Maplewood. "I can feel it pulsing through your writing, and it's exciting."

I knew what she meant but didn't pause to examine it, pushing analysis away and pledging to live in the moment. After almost twenty years as a journalist talking to others, synthesizing their experiences and doing my best to honestly relate their stories, I was now telling my own tale, and the very process of doing so pushed me to keep seeking adventures. This was key because sitting around those compounds is a fatal mistake for a newly arrived expat. In the middle of the day, they become an ocean of ennui in the middle of a vibrant city.

About a month after we arrived, the same sixty-foot container that had been filled up on our little dead-end street in Maplewood pulled up in front of our Riviera house to be unloaded by an army of Chinese workers. It was humiliating to watch these guys lug in box after box labeled "toys."

The kids immediately grabbed their bikes and took off. Jacob zipped around a little too fast, while Eli plodded along a little too slowly on his training wheels. When guards ran down from their post to push him out of a stall three times on one ride, Eli looked at me with a sweet smile and said, "Good thing they have guards in China."

I was unable to liberate Eli myself because Anna was teetering behind me on a rickety Chinese bike seat that we would have scoffed at in Maplewood. She sat back there waving at anyone who looked her way. Many of the Chinese people we passed—within the compound, mostly the guards and sweet-natured lady street sweepers—looked at curly, blond-haired Anna in awe, smiling as if they had seen a magical apparition.

# CHAPTER 4

# BEAUTIFUL SORTA

I quickly saw the advantages of living in Expat Land. It was a kids' nirvana, with friends around every corner, excellent playgrounds, and far more freedom for my children to explore on their own than they had in New Jersey. Becky and I also found an easy comfort zone, with an indispensable support network of interesting, international friends helping guide one another through expat life.

It was like living in a college dorm, but with kids and money. Everyone was in the same situation, thousands of miles away from our extended families and old friends. Close friendships developed quickly, as we became one another's families, celebrating milestones, sharing holidays, and watching one another's children.

Dulwich College of Beijing had students from more than forty countries, all of which were represented in the compounds. It was common to see white-haired Swedish kids running the streets side by side with the children of the South African military attaché or the ambassador from Equatorial Guinea, both of whom were our neighbors. It was diversity of a very peculiar kind, with a sameness of status that over-whelmed the cultural differences.

Young, single expats and older empty nesters tended to live downtown, so the compounds were filled with young families at the same stage of life. Most of us were around forty with young children, and everyone was successful enough at what they did to be sent to China. Because most people in Riviera were on an expat package, there was an overriding sense of equality. We all lived the same fake rich lifestyle, with daily domestic help, drivers, and kids in private schools.

In the United States, investment bankers, teachers, military officers, journalists, diplomats, economists, analysts, oil company executives, geologists, government civil servants, private equity investors, and GE salesmen would have lived in vastly different homes and towns. In Beijing, we all lived side by side, in the same houses, drove the same cars, and had kids attend-ing the same schools. Our circle of friends quickly became more diverse in broader ways as well; we had never hung out with so many people who attended church every Sunday or who had a wide range of political views. None of these things mattered.

We all met up every Saturday morning on the soccer pitch as our kids played in the Sports Beijing program, which became an important social outlet, helping all of us feel more rooted. The kids bonded with schoolmates and neighbors, while coaching Jacob and Eli's teams made my presence in Beijing matter to more than my family. I was paired with Scott Kronick, a native of Flint, Michigan, who had been in Beijing for fifteen years and who became one of my best friends.

Together, we plotted to keep up with the soccer-mad Eu-ropeans and to communicate with our team, which always included at least one player who spoke little or no English. I quickly wore out my German, French, and Korean vocabularies, limited to about four words each.

While I had fun wrestling with all this, Becky watched Anna run around the track and hung out with other parents in a thriving social scene. We cemented friendships that would last throughout our stay. With so few attachments and responsibilities, everyone was open to meeting new people. One day Becky chatted with the American mother of one of my players, a schoolmate of Jacob's. They were also China freshmen, newly arrived from a posting in Switzerland, and by the time the game ended, we had dinner plans. By the end of the night, we had terrific new friends. Nothing ever happened that spontaneously in New Jersey, where plans always seemed to be scheduled a month in advance.

For Becky, Beijing proved to be an ideal place to work hard and play hard. It was a place where you could text a friend to see if you could get together at the last moment. She was fond of quoting our friend Jim McGregor, a former *Wall Street Journal* bureau chief who welcomed us to Beijing with these words: "This is a place where adults can still have fun." We were all freed from things that took so much time back home: yard work, home maintenance, cooking, cleaning, harried commutes. Though she worked long hours, Becky suddenly had time to really get to know people—time she didn't have in New Jersey, where balancing family life, a demanding job, and an hour-long commute was a full-time juggling act that left little room for anything else.

HAVING A STAFF was wonderful—primarily because of all the time it freed up—but it also took some getting used to. I was suddenly an employer running a small shop, overseeing two and a half employees—a cook and a house *ayi* we inherited from Rebecca's predecessor and a third *ayi* we hired primarily to take care of Anna.

One day I walked into the kitchen to get a glass of water and the whole staff was there. Mr. Li, the cook, was sitting at the table, groceries by his side, reading glasses perched on the end of his nose, checking his expenses. Yu Ying Ayi was standing at an ironing board folding laundry. Ding Ayi was spooning yogurt into Anna's mouth.

There were all kinds of bizarre dynamics between the three of them that I vaguely knew about but willfully ignored. One *ayi* was a Beijing native who had graduated from high school, and she could apparently be brutal to the other, a rural, illiterate peasant whom the other Chinese staff considered lazy. They remained pleasant to one another in front of us, but Kathy Chen knew the real scoop and said that we were making a mistake by not making clearly delineated job descriptions.

She was probably right, but I couldn't bring myself to get too involved, because overseeing a domestic staff felt weird, stilted, and uncomfortable. People in the United States thought that the Chinese were gearing up to bury us, but we were living like nineteenth-century British tea plantation overseers in India.

To compensate for our mixed feelings, we grossly overpaid everyone, making us either very kind employers or total patsies. We had paid everyone what they asked for: 25–50 percent more than the standard rate, which still added up to about half of what we paid a single nanny at home. I realized just how cushy the Monday–Friday nine-to-five jobs working for us were when I asked the nice young girl who worked at the nearby expat grocery store if she ever got a day off, since she was there every time I shopped. "Yes," she replied with a smile. "Two days a month."

Some of our neighbors considered our household under-staffed because we did not have help before 9:00 a.m., after 6:00 p.m., or on weekends. When Becky went to Taiwan for a couple of days, I struggled getting all three children to school each morning. I had to let Jacob ride off by himself and accept that Eli and Anna would be late. I got them up, dressed, fed, cleaned, and out the door, with lunches and completed home-work in their backpacks by myself. To me, that was just basic parenting, but others thought I was crazy.

I ran into a veteran expat on the playground leaving school and related my frenzied morning.

"Why didn't your *ayi*s help?"

"They don't start this early."

"Well, change that or hire another *ayi* just for the morning."

"No, we're not used to that. We don't need another person buzzing around our house at seven a.m."

"Get over it."

We didn't want to get over it, in part because those some-times-difficult morning hours were also solid family time.


THERE WERE DANGERS to compound life as well. You are removed and living in a bubble, which whole crews of expats never pierce, spending all their time being driven around with one another, rarely interacting with any Chinese person not on their payroll. I was determined not to let that happen to us.

Every weekend, we tried to get the kids out of Expat Land, which extended to the international schools that the Chinese government banned their citizens from attending. The need to get into the real China more was reinforced on an early trip to Fundazzle and that legendary ball pit. Eli ran up to us per-plexed. "Hey," he said. "Everyone here is Chinese."

When we visited the Beijing Zoo, I anticipated the decrepit concrete cages and sad-looking animals, but I was surprised to discover that our three blue-eyed, light-haired children were prime attractions. People were staring at us, pointing, whispering, and smiling. Two-year-old Anna and her giant liquid blue eyes and tousled hair elicited the most reaction, but her brothers were also crowd pleasers. At the monkey house, three people touched Eli's hand and face, which he surprisingly didn't mind. Jacob recoiled when several people reached out to touch his impressive shock of curly blond hair.

We bought ice cream and as we sat eating our cones, a whole family stood right in front of us, gawking. The father, a cigarette dangling out of his mouth, was joyously laughing and trying to talk to Anna. He approached me, asking something in loud, fast Chinese and wildly talking with his hands. I nodded my head, correctly guessing he was asking for permission to take a picture of my daughter.

He shoved his four-year-old over to stand awkwardly next to Anna, took the picture, thanked us, and walked away grinning.

Two ladies stepped forward and asked to take a picture, speaking English, again clicking away, then thanking us profusely. A large crowd now surrounded us in an ever-growing ring. We had our backs against a wrought-iron fence, as people pointed and took pictures. Eli laughed. Anna was sheepish but unfazed. Jacob was starting to freak out. "Let's get out of here," he whispered in my ear. We rose and walked away, smiling and waving.

Moments later, an old, grizzled man in a Chinese army jacket looked my kids over, then turned to me and counted on his fingers, "Eee, Ahr, Sun" (1–2–3), before smiling wide, giving me a thumbs-up, and coming over to warmly shake my hand and pat me on the back.

I tried to explain to the kids why we were such big attractions, telling them that we simply looked different, and explaining China's one-child policy and how that made a three-child family a special sight. As soon as I said, "In China, people are only allowed to have one kid," Eli's eyes grew fearful; I understood that he was worried that we were going to have to get rid of him and Anna. "That's only for Chinese people," I quickly added.

Clearly, we all had a lot to learn.

We kept pushing out, sometimes even prompted by the kids. One day, Jacob came home from second grade perplexed.

"Why haven't we been to the Forbidden City or Tiananmen Square?" he asked. "They are two of the most visited, famous tourist sites in the world."

We headed for Tiananmen that weekend, drawing attention the moment we arrived. Rural residents were always particularly interested in our family, and Tiananmen, like the zoo, was filled with Chinese tourists. Whole tour groups clad in matching red baseball hats followed us, waving, smiling, counting up our three kids with glee and repeatedly snapping pictures of Anna. She was becoming a popular cell-phone wallpaper.

Jacob was fascinated by massive statues made from potted flowers depicting various balls used in Olympic sports—ping-pong, tennis, volleyball, and soccer, with the Olympic "One World, One Dream" logo spelled out in giant letters, in both English and Chinese. I wanted to draw everyone's attention to another Olympic marker. Across a wide boulevard, in front of one of the many monolithic government buildings that surround the square, was a clock counting down the days until the 8-8-08 Opening Ceremony. It read 1,046.

"That," I said to my family, pointing across the street, "is how many days we have left in China."

It seemed like an awfully big number.

# CHAPTER 5

# SAY WHAT?

On one of my first days in Beijing, I listened to Kathy Chen and Mr. Dou engage in an animated conversation with dumbfounded admiration for any foreigner who could master Mandarin. I heard no words—just a series of guttural sounds. The experience left me shaken, simultaneously determined to learn Chinese and questioning whether I could ever do so. It felt like I had as much chance of learning how to communicate with dolphins.

I decided to follow the lead of Theo Yardley, my neighbor, friend, and China guide who spoke the language brilliantly. I enrolled in twice-a-week, two-hour classes at her downtown language school, which was popular with journalists and embassy employees. I was paired with two French women. After struggling through two classes, I longed for a friend to share this crazy experience with.

The next week, Theo talked me into attending a welcome coffee in our compound clubhouse. I put up a fight, certain that I would be the only man there. But as soon as I walked in, the chipper Australian chairwoman of the welcome committee grabbed me by the arm and dragged me across the room, past packs of women sipping coffee and eating "biscuits." Finding her prey, she triumphantly introduced me to Tom Davis, the only other male trailing spouse anyone knew about. She had correctly guessed we would be happy to see each other.

Tom had also quit his job—as a Seattle insurance under-writer—to move to Beijing when his wife received a promo-tion. We were thrown together by circumstance, and my initial impression was that I didn't have much in common with this dry, quiet bespectacled Montana native.

But Tom's face lit up when I told him about the Papa John's–sponsored expat softball team I had stumbled onto, and I prom-ised to see if I could get him on. Tom was by my side a few days later when we returned for a doubleheader at a still-unfinished compound just down the road from Riviera. The field looked spectacular, with a well-manicured outfield and a glistening brown infield, but it felt completely wrong. The infield was topped by several inches of loose, soft dirt. It was clearly the work of people who had studied pictures of a baseball field but had never actually stood on one.

After squeaking out one win over a Chinese team and getting clobbered by a U.S. Embassy squad led by Marines with bulg-ing, tattooed biceps, Tom and I walked home together. Both slightly unsteady on hamstrings tweaked by running through the sand, we laughed about the field and how it seemed like an apt metaphor for China, where many things were not quite what they seemed. When Tom said he was looking for a Chi-nese class, I smiled and said I had him covered.


TOM'S WIFE, CATHY, had a company driver who dropped her at work then came back to take us to class. Chatting in the back of that Buick minivan during our regular commute, we realized that we shared many of the same passions, talking effortlessly about the mountains of the American West, fatherhood, World War II history, and the Pittsburgh Steelers. He had fallen in love with my hometown football team as a kid in a Montana mining town, relating to their blue-collar appeal.

I began looking forward to these rides, and the more I got to know Tom, the more impressed I was. He and Cathy had two daughters, Shealyn, then five, and Sudha, four. They adopted the latter from India knowing that a birth defect necessitated the amputation of both her feet. I thought this elevated them to sainthood, but Tom was very matter-of-fact about it.

"They don't ask you to adopt a disabled child right away," he explained. "It is a long process and first they decide you can probably handle it and then they introduce the idea."

We spoke often of going on more outings together—we were particularly excited about hiking on the Great Wall—but Tom was fully committed to being home when his girls got off the school bus every day at noon. This was almost a quaint notion here, in the land of *ayi*s.

MANDARIN HAS FOUR tones, and the right word said with the wrong tone, or inflection, can have a radically different meaning. So it made sense for the school to spend many hours merely practicing the proper expression of tones before teaching any vocabulary. It also made for some gruesomely boring lessons. We rotated through cubicles and teachers, many of them young women looking at us blankly as we grew exasperated. Some seemed intent on having us mimic not only their pronunciation but also their pitch.

We spent entire classes saying "taaaa" in an absurdly high

voice, though I was sure that my goal was not to sound like a twenty-two-year-old Chinese woman. Then, one day Tom and I walked into a small classroom and found a quiet, studious young man with a brush cut sitting behind the desk. He seemed at once more serious and less rigid than anyone else we had encountered, and we immediately felt more relaxed and confident.

Yechen, who was twenty-nine, had just returned from five years teaching at a prestigious British university, so he spoke much better English than his colleagues. He was also happy to toss the syllabus and intuitively guide us into a comfort zone. He jumped back and forth in the book so we could start learning some vocabulary, and when one of us stalled on a sound, he moved on, instead of hammering us with our failures, as the others did.

I hired Yechen to translate a *Slam* interview with basketball player Sun Yue. As soon as we climbed into a cab, Yechen told me that he hated the school and would soon be quitting. Tom and I hired him, and we began private lessons at my dining room table a few weeks later.

Yechen said he was going to start over from square one and he was going to teach us characters, insisting that you can't really understand Chinese language or culture without them. He brought in textbooks from the British university. He also suggested we get out and interact with people as much as possible, soaking in the language and getting more of a feel for its natural usage. This was easy for me, as I was already eagerly exploring both downtown and my immediate semirural neighborhood.

I often rode my bike over to a village just a quarter mile outside the back gate of our compound. Riding in, I passed a run-down supermarket, a meat store, and a couple of produce stands, where I began shopping, buying huge bags of apples, pears, navel oranges, bananas, and tiny clementines, as well as fresh tofu, noodles, eggplant, cilantro, and mushrooms—all for about five dollars.

Across the street was a tiny restaurant, little more than a couple of oil drums with stools under a billowing tent. Eventually, I would work up my nerve to try that place, which served delicious, crispy egg pancakes. I would also discover that the grocery store had a small hot food place that made great pork and chive dumplings, steamed buns, and simple flat breads. But I was nervous the first time I ate in the village and so limited myself to considering the two real restaurants.

I wandered into one, finding it empty at 2:00 p.m., normal for a working-class Chinese restaurant, where most people eat lunch at noon on the dot. Two lounging waitresses looked at me with surprise, then rushed over with a one-page handwritten menu. Unable to read it, or to use the point-and-nod ordering technique I had already perfected since no one was there, I just ordered noodles, because it was safe and was one of the only foods I could say properly.

The waitresses kept asking me about what kind of noodles I wanted, and I kept answering, "*Wo budong—zhe mian.*" (I don't understand—just noodles.) I was speaking single-word, illiterate Chinese, and we were all laughing as they pantomimed all sorts of things. The only thing I could really make out was someone hand-pulling noodles, so I just kept saying "*dui, dui*" (right, right).

After consulting each other, one waitress retreated to the kitchen and the other brought me tea, then hovered nearby. I smiled at her. She smiled back, then pointed to the table and said, in remarkably unaccented English, "Desk."

"*Bu desk* (not desk)," I said. "Table."

Puzzled, she brought over her pen and pad and handed them to me. I wrote "table," which she looked at and read, quite clearly: "Table."

I took the pad and wrote the following:

**Chair**

**Cup**

**Tea**

**Noodles**

**Me**

**You**

**Alan**

She read them all out loud as I pointed to the appropriate object. All Chinese study English in school and many who cannot confidently say a single word can read and write quite well, but I did not know this yet.

The cook poked his head out of the kitchen and stared as the other waitress emerged and placed a large steaming bowl of dark brown broth in front of me. I smiled and stirred the soup with my chopsticks. At the bottom was a large serving of fresh, flat noodles. I said, "*Hen hao*" (very good) and started eating. It was simple, tasty food.

The broth had a few pieces of stew meat bobbing around some tasty fresh greens, and the noodles were freshly made, something I would quickly get used to in China. A few sprigs of cilantro floated around the top.

A middle-aged man in a long green army coat wandered in to smoke, sip tea, and stare at me as I ate. I waved off the cigarette he offered and listened, uncomprehending, as he spoke at length, ignoring my insistence that I didn't understand him.

I smiled and nodded while slurping down the noodles, then picked up the bowl to drink the soup, leaving most of the chunky pieces of mystery meat at the bottom.

My pupil cleared my place, then returned with her sheet. I wrote out more words, as several more people wandered in. I now had a small class, and everyone laughed when one of them called me "*laoshi*" (teacher). I was writing down every object I could see, then reading the words aloud and pointing.

"Bowl . . . television . . . spoon . . . shirt . . . clock . . . shoes . . . pants."

The first waitress could read the English perfectly and grew more proud and excited with each properly executed word. Everyone else watched and listened.

Eventually, I picked up the bill, paid 3 RMB (about 40 cents) and rose to leave, saying, "*Xie Xie. Zai jian.*" (Thank you. Good-bye.)

My star pupil proudly responded in English: "You're welcome. Thank you. Good-bye."

Wobbling home on my bike, the handlebars tipsy with bags of produce, I felt at peace and full of wonder, excited that such a place was so close at hand. Pulling back onto the main road behind Riviera, I saw the turnoff to the baseball diamond, which seemed like a crossroads between chasing a mirage and living in the here and now.

I had already met expats who spent most of their time trying to re-create their home life in China, and they were often seething with complaints and disappointments. Like that baseball field, things would never be quite right for them; the best they could achieve was a second-rate imitation. Thriving expats accepted life in China for what it was and tried to take advantage of it all. I knew what my choice would be.

# CHAPTER 6

# KEY TO THE HIGHWAY

**W**e began the process of getting our driver's licenses almost immediately after arriving in China. It was maddening to be stranded in a suburban compound, unable to drive for the first time in twenty-three years—particularly since we had a free car waiting for us. The bureau's 1992 Beijing Jeep Cherokee would never be replaced and probably should have been retired long ago, but its presence in front of the house was a tease.

I took it out for a few spins around the Riviera. The clutch balked, and the dead shocks allowed each of the compound's many speed bumps to rattle my innards, but I wanted to drive it in the worst way. Unfortunately, there was no shortcut to getting a license.

Many of my friends and neighbors had family drivers, often paid for by their employers. Some companies actually prohibited their employees from driving at all, because of liability fears. Rebecca had Mr. Dou, a company driver who usually took her to and from work. But we were otherwise on our own.

Sick of waiting a half an hour for a cab to take me a mile,

I gave in to temptation and started driving the Jeep. We restricted our outings to nearby places but that still meant cruising up and down Jing Shun Lu, the crazy, busy road that some longtime expats had dubbed "blood alley."

The basic rule of Chinese driving seemed to be: never stop unless you absolutely must. If there's the slightest opening, a car will try to slip through. If there is a sliver between vehicles on a pulsing, busy thoroughfare, a line of cars will turn left into the teeth of swarming traffic in a frantic game of chicken. Driving in Beijing is a full-body experience, one that I actually enjoyed from the start. You feel alive behind the wheel, maybe because of the very real possibility that you could soon be dead.

For all the hyperaggressive drivers—including chauffeured German sedans moving at hyperspeed—the roads were also clogged with slow-moving vehicles. These included souped-up tractors dragging enormous, overhanging payloads and cars piloted by nervous, freshly minted drivers. In a few years, Beijing had gone from busting with bikes to crowded with cars, and the result was countless inexperienced drivers who drove at half the speed limit.

We quickly got used to navigating this morass, and the undertow of guilt and panic we felt about unlicensed driving began to ebb. Then one night we drove up to meet friends, including one U.S. Embassy official who knew China well.

"You are crazy to drive without a license," he said. "If you get into a small accident, it is going to cost you a lot of money. If you get into a bad one and someone is hurt or killed, at best you will have your visas taken away and have to leave the country. At worst, you'll end up in jail."

It's easy to feel above the law living in a foreign culture, so I applied a simple rule that I would turn to regularly in coming years: just imagine the reverse situation. I pictured an unlicensed Chinese national mowing down an American kid and imagined the uproar that would follow. Besides, we had only been in China for a month and things were going impossibly well. Rolling the dice like this was foolish. We stopped driving and dove into the long process of getting our licenses.

To BEGIN, MR. Dou drove us thirty minutes south to a hulking bureaucratic building, grandly labeled "People's Republic of China Office of Traffic Safety Compliance and Road Rules." To the left of the main door another entrance read "Foreigner License." Mr. Dou filled out countless papers, handed over a stack of passport-sized photos, and called us up to sign a few things, before handing us study books and telling us that the next available appointment was in three weeks.

On the way back, we began looking over the books and started getting concerned. The book included 750 questions, all in badly translated "Chinglish" that required careful reading. We would have to correctly answer 90 out of 100, randomly selected by a computer. About half were obvious and another 25 percent were fathomable, which left 25 percent you simply had to memorize, because they made little sense.

> For an open abdominal wound, such as protrusion of the small intestine tube, we should:
>
> a.  put it back.
> b.  no treatment.
> c.  not put it back, but cover it with a bowl or jar, and bind the bowl or jar with a cloth belt.

The answer is C.

There were also fifty questions about penalties, fines, and points docked for various offenses, few of which were intuitive.

When a driver on probation drives vehicles loaded with explosive goods, inflammable and explosive chemical goods, highly toxic goods or radioactive dangerous goods, the penalty is __ points for each violation.

The choices were 1, 2, or 3 and the answer was 2, the same as talking on a cell phone while driving. I could only hope that probationary drivers driving "radioactive dangerous goods" are less common than the ubiquitous driving while chatting.

THREE WEEKS LATER, we crammed in the backseat of Mr. Dou's car on our way to the test. When we arrived, we were ushered upstairs with a group of twenty-five, entering a large room proctored by five uniformed police officers. I chose English from twelve language options, instructions popped up, and a little clock in the upper right corner began counting down my forty-five minutes.

I guessed on three of the first fifteen questions and realized that my odds of survival were low. I felt like the walking dead. I was moving too quickly through the test, sure that the ones I didn't know wouldn't benefit from extra analysis.

A frowning red face appeared as soon as I hit send without rechecking any answers. A cop shooed me to the front, where an unsmiling woman officer scribbled "82" on the bottom of my form and handed it back. I actually thought that was pretty good.

Downstairs, I handed my paper to Mr. Dou, who frowned and shook his head with a look that could have indicated either pity or disgust. All my hopes were pinned on Becky. If she got her license, at least we could use the car right away. One person after another emerged, most of them frowning, before my wife finally walked out, looking despondent. She had scored an 87. The next available appointment was in three weeks.

We drove back to town in dejected silence. While Rebecca went to work, where she had to swallow her pride and admit failure, I headed for a sports bar to watch the Steelers on *Sunday Night Football* (Monday morning in China). Ten a.m. wasn't too early for a pint of Guinness, which helped sweep me away to another world. As much as I was digging China, sometimes I needed a dose of Pittsburgh, and nothing provided it quite like my beloved Steelers.

THREE WEEKS LATER, we again walked into the licensing bureau, just as the previous hour's test takers were coming downstairs. A beefy American guy in a Carhartt jacket approached his driver, who was standing next to me. "I am not coming here again, no matter what," he said, in a thick southern accent. "Do you understand? I am not taking this test again. No way, no how. I will just hire cabs and drivers. This is ridiculous."

He was looking at me, clearly wanting someone to feel his pain. He said he was from Tennessee, here with five other guys to install giant turbine engines all over the country.

"The first four guys came in here and flunked, so us two have been studying our asses off for three days," he recounted. "I got an 87. This is ridiculous."

He grunted when I said that people were making fun of us for failing—my blog was ablaze with flaming posts. "Show them this damn book." He waved it around. "Then see who's laughing."

Every Chinese person we discussed our failure with had been far less sympathetic, finding our difficulties laughable. Each of them had scored between 95 and 100 on the test; they considered this kind of straight memorization to be child's play.

Upstairs in the test room, my confidence returned as I breezed through the first fifteen questions. I finished, reviewed my answers, changed three, and hit "Done." A dancing smiley face immediately appeared. I had scored a 90. I felt like jumping up and spiking my study book.

I gave Rebecca a thumbs-up, mouthed "good luck," and walked out grinning. Another guy entered the stairs with me, also smiling maniacally. When I congratulated him, he answered with a thick Eastern European accent.

"I went to four years of university and many more of advance degree study but I have never stayed up all night studying until last night. This test is unbelievable!" It was his second time taking the exam as well. I told him we should celebrate tonight.

"We must, we must!" He patted me on the back and shook my hand. "This is a great day."

Downstairs, I handed my paper to Mr. Dou, who smiled. He kept asking about Rebecca, apparently wondering if we had shared answers, not understanding that was impossible. We both waited anxiously for ten minutes until she emerged with a big smile. She had scored a 94.

As we walked back to the car holding hands, I told Becky that I didn't remember feeling such joy since our kids were born. It must have been an exaggeration, but she did not disagree. She had saved some serious face in the office, where her large Chinese staff was waiting to see whether or not the new boss had failed again.

# CHAPTER 7

# WHEN YOU FEEL IT, YOU KNOW

With our driver's licenses in hand and things falling into place, I was able to concentrate on smaller pleasures, like finding someone to play music with. I had come to Beijing with high hopes of establishing myself as a musician rather than a musical observer.

I had always been tentative playing guitar around my family and friends, because they didn't think of me as a musician, and around others because they often expected me to be great due to my long association with *Guitar World*. Singing in public was even harder. I overcame some of these insecurities when I joined a friend's band for three songs at a big farewell party before we left for China, and I hoped to build on that in Beijing. Since no one knew I didn't sing, I could sing.

Despite playing for fifteen years, I had not advanced beyond solid intermediate status. I had been listening to music with serious intent since I was twelve, but didn't really start playing guitar until I became *Guitar World* managing editor at age twenty-four. I took just enough guitar lessons to allow intelligent conversations with both my colleagues and the many guitarists I interviewed for the magazine, which we were establishing as one of the country's top music magazines filled with in-depth features that gave me tremendous access.

These meetings were consistently thrilling; *Guitar World* offered me fly-on-the-wall access to many of the musicians I admired most. I ate lunch with blues greats B.B. King and Buddy Guy and listened to them discuss how much it pained them to see "them kids" smash up guitars, the very things that had given them so much. I met with Eric Clapton in his hotel suite; got drunk with Metallica's James Hetfield years before he made a well-documented trip to rehab; interviewed Albert King, my favorite blues guitarist, backstage just months before he died; sat in on many recording and rehearsal sessions; and watched the Allman Brothers Band perform from a perch behind Gregg Allman's organ.

Being close to the music—not the celebrity, but the *music*—was invaluable, and I couldn't imagine giving it up, even when some of my family and friends thought I was slumming. I was fulfilling a childhood vision I first had as a twelve year old spending hours lying on my brother's yellow shag carpeting listening to the Allman Brothers Band's *Eat a Peach* and studying the psychedelic artwork inside the double album's gatefold.

In eighth-grade English class I chose the late guitarist Duane Allman as the subject of my biography of a great American. Duane had died in a 1971 motorcycle crash at age twenty-four, when I was five years old. My teacher returned the paper with two grades: an A and an incomplete with a note to see her. "This is very good," she said. "Frankly, it's hard for me to be-lieve you wrote it by yourself. Did your brother lend a hand?"

. . . .

TWENTY YEARS LATER I was writing historical essays about the band for Allman Brothers' CD releases. It felt natural, but had I followed my passion or simply taken the path of least resistance? I had ended up with a career I knew I could do in junior high.

My deep immersion in music and my experiences with great musicians actually made me take my own guitar playing less seriously—why bother if I couldn't live up to my heroes' standards? Having a collaborator with whom I felt the spark of inspiration could break this feeling. I had several over the years, and my playing improved in radical leaps during these periods. Otherwise, I stagnated despite good instincts because I found playing music by myself uninspiring and boring. The potential for something exciting, maybe even transcendent, existed only in the interaction with others, and I never knew where I might find that inspiration.

The most knowledgeable, helpful poster on the *Guitar World Online* message boards was "Tragocaster," a Michigan guitarist who persistently invited me to his Sunday night gigs at the rural Otisville Hotel. I finally took him up on it one summer night while visiting Becky's family in Bay City. My father-in-law insisted on joining me for the hour-long drive down a dark two-lane road. Just after the Otisville town limits sign, the shoulder of the road became filled with Harley-Davidsons. The ramshackle wood frame hotel sat at the town's only intersection and was completely surrounded by the big bikes.

Clusters of bikers congregated in front wearing leather vests showing gang colors, their long beards spilling down over bulging bellies. Harold and I parked his cherry red VW bug around the corner and sat talking.

"I'm sorry," I said. "I had no idea this was a biker bar. We can go home. I won't be mad."

"No," he said. "It will be fun. I haven't been to a place like this in years."

We walked up the steps—Harold in his khaki shorts pulled halfway up his gut, black socks leading to loafers. He strolled right through the packed crowd of beefy bikers and bought two Buds before we found a spot at a table. As I relaxed about the crowd, I grew nervous in an entirely different way—I was going to be in way over my head with the great Buick City Blues Band.

But Trag was a gracious, terrific bandleader, pulling me into the music and never showing me up—traits I would try to mimic with my own band years later. I played the entire set, and over the next three years I headed for Otisville any time we were in Michigan on a Sunday night. My in-laws thought it was crazy to drive down a dark two-lane highway for a hundred miles to hang out until 2:00 a.m. in a rickety roadhouse where fights occasionally erupted. But Becky never complained because she understood how much I loved those jams.

Finding a place like that in Beijing seemed unlikely, but I kept hoping to stumble onto a great musical partner. During my first week, I heard the sound of guitars drifting out of a second-floor window of the compound clubhouse. I left my family, following the faint sound of a solid folk rock groove up the curving central stairway and down a hallway. Inside a large room I found four Western guys rocking out in front of rows of empty folding chairs. When I asked a woman standing in the back when the show was, she shot me a confused look. "They're rehearsing for this morning's worship service." I briefly pondered whether they'd let a Jewish guy into their contemporary Christian rock band before moving on.

When our sea shipment arrived, I quickly found my Vox amp and trusty Fender Stratocaster. I plugged the amp into an adapter and popped it into the wall. The red light glowed warmly as I hit a single E chord, which rang for a split second before the light faded and the amp powered off with an ugly sizzle. I had made a classic rookie mistake, using an adapter when I needed a transformer to step my American 110-volt amp up to the Chinese 220. I slid the silenced amp over by my desk, where it would gather dust for a year.

A few months later, I heard about a downtown club featuring Sunday night jam sessions led by Chicago blues musicians on monthlong residencies. I put new strings on my Strat, only to learn that the club was on the verge of folding and the music was done. I didn't touch my guitar for months.

One night I was sitting in the Orchard, my favorite local restaurant, sipping a beer and listening to a jazz band. The music was mediocre but the setting was superb. The Orchard was a refuge, sitting on a lake surrounded by a thousand apple and pear trees, with a luxuriant, serene garden in the back.

The owners, Lisa Minder and Ertao Wu, were an American/Chinese couple, and the place, which they designed and built themselves, reflected their diverse backgrounds. The food was Western, and the eclectic, understated design mixed European, American, and Chinese furniture under exposed beams made of reclaimed timber.

I told Lisa, a native of Wheeling, West Virginia, that it was nice to hear live music so close to home. "Eh, I'm sick of jazz," she replied. "Don't you play guitar? How about hosting an acoustic open mic night?"

She had a vision of expats pulling mandolins and banjos out of their closets. I told her I'd love to do it if I found a partner, but I wasn't comfortable performing solo.

Shortly after, I had a single fun jam session with a friend of a friend. I asked if he'd like to host that open mic with me, but he only wanted to perform at the Orchard with his own group. I booked it for him, joining at the end of the night for three songs.

Afterward, Lisa told me how much she enjoyed the music, especially my singing, a compliment all the more satisfying for being so surprising.

"I'd still like you to host an open mic," she said.

I had a gig. I just needed a band.

# CHAPTER 8

# INTO THE GREAT WIDE OPEN

There are countless motivations for traveling, but most people abandon "throwing yourself into the deep end to see if you can swim" after they have kids. It just feels too risky to set off on aimless wanderings into parts unknown with children in tow.

Yet kids, too, can tap into something deep within themselves when forced to stretch beyond their comfort zones, which we began realizing as soon as we took our first trip into China's vast, beautiful, and underdeveloped interior. These journeys were far more adventurous than anything we would have attempted at home.

China had three weeklong holidays when virtually the entire country shuts down: the first week of October, the first week of May, and Chinese New Year, which varies with the lunar calendar. These breaks are prime times to go exploring, but because 1.3 billion other people have the same idea, many expats prefer to stay put or leave the country, lighting out for Thailand, Malaysia, or other Asian ports of call. We ignored this line of thinking, visiting the southern towns of Guilin and

Yangshuo for our first October holiday, just six weeks after we arrived in China.

We knew little about the places, except that a friend said they were beautiful and guidebooks showed wondrous limestone hilltops covered in dense green foliage rising above the picturesque Li River. In Guilin, we floated down the river, saw cormorant fishermen operating in the ancient way, visited caves packed with Chinese tourists, and watched Anna's photo being taken dozens of times.

Our guide "Judy" took us for two dinners at the Asia Pacific restaurant, because, she said, it was the cleanest, most air-conditioned place in town. We were mostly focused on the veritable petting zoo in the front, where diners could choose their meal, selecting from dozens of aquatic tanks of critters, as well as wood cages filled with pheasants and large muskrat-like rodents. A separate nook contained several large glass terrariums filled with stacks of writhing snakes, which made Becky's skin crawl and sent her rushing back to the table to drink tea while the kids and I looked over the animals and watched other guests select a fowl and haggle over the price. I tried to rush my children away before the bird could be killed, but they understood exactly what was about to happen and wanted to witness it. It didn't seem to hurt their appetite at all as we sat down for scallion pancakes, sautéed chicken, and succulent boiled river shrimp.

We passed dozens of roadside noodle stands, which Judy told me were "Guilin rice noodles, the traditional local food." Surprised that I wanted to try these, she took us to a nice little restaurant where I slurped down a bowl that cost about 16 cents. Eli and Anna also loved the fresh noodles, adding the peanuts and cilantro just as Becky and I did, but skipping the hot sauce. Jacob ate granola bars and sorted Pokémon cards in the van.

But the real discovery took place on the bumpy dirt roads outside Yangshuo, a few hours south of Guilin. "Peggy," the local guide we had hired, spoke in a nonstop patter of Chinglish, with us catching maybe 20 percent. She marched us up to a bike rental place and asked for a kid's seat. The young lady running the stand smiled, nodded, and pulled out a wicker basket, which she strapped to the back of a tandem bike with some wire. There was no way to close the front, but she waved away our concern, motioning for us to put Anna in, then taking a sheet and tying a knot in front of our daughter.

Anna would be fine, as long as she consented to stay there. If she fussed at all, this jury-rigged contraption would not work. She was on the back of a tandem piloted by Becky and Jacob, because Eli, at five, was strapped into a similar chair behind me, his knees hitting me in the back; he was too big for the seat, but too small to pedal any of their bikes.

We set out like this across a beautiful, otherworldly landscape. Deep in the country, we stopped for lunch at a tiny restaurant with a small English translation menu. We ordered "fresh local chicken," and I believed the menu's words because several birds ran wild through the garden behind our picnic table. Jacob munched on white rice and French fries. When the chicken came out, it was a whole bird chopped up and piled on a plate, with the feet on top. Eli pushed them aside and dug into a delicious ginger-infused meal. We capped it off with ice cream bars, which we came to regard as an essential food group on these outings, since making sure our kids didn't melt down from hunger became more important than worrying about their diets.

Eli was taken aback by his first meeting with squat toilets. We were deep in the countryside and Peggy asked some local people if we could use their facilities. I took Eli into the toilet.

He looked at the hole in the ground and asked me where "their other toilet" was. "This is it," I said.

"No, seriously," he insisted. "The real one. To use for number two."

"Seriously, this is it," I said. "They use it for everything."

He was awed, but Anna was unaffected. She had been on the edge of toilet training, and we realized she was all the way there when she did not resort to diapers on this trip. This required Becky and I to each become adept at stripping Anna down and holding her up in the air over a toilet hole without looking down; doing so might have buckled our knees.

WHEN THE MAY holiday rolled around, we were ready for another China adventure, but wanted to steer far enough off the beaten path to avoid huge crowds. On a *WSJ* colleague's recommendation, we chose the south-central province of Guizhou, a remote, river-filled place dotted with ethnic minority villages set on high mountains.

It was not an obvious destination. As China's poorest province, with a per capita income of $614, Guizhou lacked many amenities a vacationing family might seek—swimming pools, tourist sites like caves, even established hiking or biking trails of the sort we enjoyed in Yangshuo. Few people we knew had been there. The expat-oriented travel agent first tried to correct me, then laughed out loud when I insisted on buying air tickets to the capital of Guiyang.

We spent one night there, having our first taste of local food, which was different from any other Chinese cuisine I had tasted, its extreme spiciness balanced by sour, pickled vegetables, cilantro, and other fresh herbs. The revelatory food was consistently excellent throughout the province, even at dumpy restaurants in tiny towns. We became regulars at several Bei-jing Guizhou restaurants for the rest of our stay in China.

"We say if it doesn't have chilies, it's not food," said our guide Huang Duan ("Call me Howard"). As a lifelong hot food devotee, I felt like I had found my tribe, but in most re-spects, it felt as if we were at the end of the world.

A growing pack of curious onlookers followed us from our hotel to the restaurant in Guiyang, and the entire waitstaff crowded around two-and-a-half-year-old Anna, wanting to hold her, kiss her, and pose for pictures with her. This ritual would be repeated over and over during our visit; Gandalf the White wizard could not have received more amazed stares had he appeared on the streets of Guizhou.

"Many of these people have never seen anyone who looks like Anna, except in pictures," Huang Duan explained. "They think she looks like an angel."

The next day we drove three hours to the mountain outpost of Kaili, a much smaller, poorer, and dirtier city, which is the capital of the "Miao and Dong (minority groups) Autonomous Prefecture." China has fifty-five recognized minority groups, officially making up about 9 percent of the population. The Miao are known as Hmong in Laos and other parts of Asia and have a sizable population in the United States.

We bumped over rutted roads in this rough coal-mining region, taking in scenes of slag and ash heaps and bustling mines. I wondered what we had gotten ourselves into, but then we drove through deep green mountains, with even the steep-est slopes covered in terraced rice paddies. Men plowed the muddy fields behind water buffalo. Women chopped tall grass with handheld scythes, loading it into large wire baskets bal-anced on either end of a long wooden pole carried across their shoulders.

It was fascinating and beautiful, but as the day wore on, the kids wilted in the rising heat as we bounced from one village to another. By the time we climbed into the van for the bumpy, sweaty ride back from a ramshackle village where we bought batik purses and jackets, we were worn out, the kids were restless, and I wondered if we could keep up this pace for three more days. Chinese tour guides seemed to think that they were not doing their job if they did not rush you to as many places as possible each day. We were passing through remarkable countryside, but not really stopping to explore it, sticking instead to a steady litany of villages, which were fascinating but beginning to run together, especially for the kids.

Our anxiety deepened during dinner at a stuffy, un–air-conditioned restaurant. Huang Duan ordered our food, then ran out to get us cold beer and soda when the waitress said they did not have any. As Becky and I pulled delicious, slow-cooked ribs out of a bamboo steamer filled with moist, flavorful rice, Jacob let out a yelp. "I hate this food!" he screamed.

Eli flopped onto the old linoleum floor, where Anna joined him, much to the horror of the young waitress hovering by the door to our private room holding a pot of tea. Our children were falling apart, and it was clear that we couldn't maintain this pace for three more days.

THE NEXT MORNING, the kids ate the Trix cereal we traveled with while Rebecca and I conferred with Huang Duan over a breakfast of dumplings and spicy noodles. We told him to slash a third of each day's activities and allow time for the kids to ramble through some of the beautiful fields we were zipping by. We were forcing flexibility on our children, but we had to be a bit realistic.

We visited a large Miao village, where we joined Chinese tourists watching a traditional flute and dance show, the women clad in colorful hand-embroidered dresses. As usual, Anna's appearance drew as much attention as the little girls clad in traditional silver hats and necklaces. We bought the kids wooden swords that would get a workout over the next few days. Later we drove farther into the boonies and were the lone visitors in a remote Miao outpost, where we viewed traditional homes housing pigs, chickens, and water buffalo on the first stone floor and several generations on the top two wooden floors.

Packs of beautiful, dirty-faced kids followed us everywhere—minorities are not bound by the one-child policy—so I started filling my pockets with lollipops and gum at tiny village shops, which were usually just glass-fronted counters stocked with simple provisions like water, cigarettes, instant noodles, batteries, and candy. Jacob and Eli loved handing out the sweets. One five-year-old boy appeared with a four-inch bug on a string leash. Our kids thought that this mantis-like creature was the coolest pet they had ever seen.

The next day we told our guide to drop us off so we could hike across rice paddies and through two villages, which were off the tourist path. They were just places where people lived. As we neared a bridge that would take us back to our van, I stopped at one of those little stores to buy water and cookies for the kids. A group of village women, clad in traditional blue smocks and white head coverings, were eating lunch in a back room. One called out, *"Chi fan!" "Chi fan!"* (Eat, eat!), and waved me in. When I entered, she handed me a bowl of congee (rice porridge) and gently pushed me onto a small wooden stool. The congee tasted like glue. Looking at a sea of smiling, expectant faces, I smiled and said, *"Hao chi!"* (Tastes good!)

They pulled up another chair and handed Rebecca a bowl. Soon bowls of cooked food came our way, including some spicy mystery meat, which lent the congee a strong, vibrant taste. The kids watched the whole scene with amused smiles, while eating their "Ocop" faux Oreos—we now considered packaged cookies, reliably available anywhere, another essential food group.

We lunched at a local barbecue joint hard by the banks of the churning Bala River, underneath cloud-shrouded, deep green peaks. It was part of my plan to give the kids more freedom; the day before we had passed the place and I envisioned stone skipping and fisherman watching on its large, pebbly river beach, which would be a big improvement over forcing them to sit at a table in a gritty roadside restaurant. Our guide did not want to take us there and remained uneasy when we insisted. Becky and I laughed about how uptight he was, but the source of his discomfort soon became clear: even by rural China standards, the sanitary conditions were spotty.

You walked into a dirty little greeting area, chose some meat or fish, and then were given a private grill to cook your own food by the riverside. The whole area was muddy—no surprise since there had been a light mist or heavy rain throughout our visit. As we tentatively walked around the outdoor dining area waiting for our food, our kids started playing with a gaggle of children.

Their playmates were fellow diners as well as Miaos from a neighboring village, including one boy zipping around on a homemade scooter, which was basically just two planks of wood with rickety wheels attached. He gave each of our kids a turn. Throughout this trip Jacob and Eli made friends with fun-loving Chinese boys, getting into hardcore games of tag, karate, and Game Boy playing. There are an awful lot of wild boys in the world, and it became obvious that they can spot one another and connect without saying a word.

Anna picked up a small fish a villager had caught and swung it around by its tail, much to the delight of the other guests eating nearby, all of them tourists from a city about eight hours away. They handed us little cups of beer and insisted we sample their fresh-grilled meat and fish.

We took over a nearby gazebo and invited our new friends to join us when our food arrived. Jacob, a veritable vegetarian, was so hungry and having so much fun with his new friends that he tried marinated, grilled beef. He tentatively stuck a corner in his mouth and nibbled, as Becky and I watched intently while pretending to have no interest.

"Mmmm. This is great."

He gobbled down the piece and asked for another. He ate a whole order and has been a steak-loving carnivore ever since.

We all grilled and ate together, then the men sat in the gazebo drinking beer while the women walked down to the riverbank and oversaw the children. Becky would normally have given me a hard time about this unfair division of labor, but we were both too enchanted to want to change a thing. The kids scampered around, catching crabs, throwing rocks into the raging brown river, and playing tag.

Huang Duan, finally realizing we were happy and that he wasn't doing a bad job, joined us, eating, drinking, and serving as our translator. We lingered for hours, as I downed one tiny plastic cup of lukewarm beer after another after endless toasts of "*gan-bei*" (bottoms up). As we started to say our good-byes, four of the older village girls, all about twelve years old, swept in to take our bottles. They carefully poured the remnants of each into a two-liter soda bottle, no doubt for their parents' enjoyment, and gathered up the empties, which each had a deposit worth about a dime.

We finally said our good-byes and began slowly walking through the light mud back to our van. "Thank you, Dad," Jacob said, giving me a big hug. "This was the best lunch ever."

# CHAPTER 9

# SAD AND DEEP AS YOU

I was washing my hands early one morning when my cell phone began chirping in my pocket. Stumbling to yank it out with still-dripping hands, I fumbled and watched it skitter across the tile floor. I reached over and grabbed it, answering in a rush.

"Hello."

"Hi, Alan. It's Dad."

"Hi. How are you doing?"

"Ah, not so good. I have a little bladder C-A."

"A little what?"

"Bladder C-A. Bladder cancer. Same thing that got Doc Meyers."

Doc was a dear family friend who passed away a decade earlier. My father, too, is an old-school physician, a retired pediatrician, and it didn't surprise me to hear him speak about his own diagnosis with clinical matter-of-factness. It was the diagnosis itself that left me speechless.

"I know this is hard on you being so far away, but don't let it be," he said. "I'm fine. I'll have a little surgery, take the tumor out, biopsy it, and see what's what. Don't worry about it."

I tried to digest this mixed message: *"Don't worry about it." "It's just a little bladder C-A." "Same thing that got Doc Meyers."*

I worried.

The only good thing about this crisis is that it transformed a hard decision into a no-brainer. We had been debating the wisdom of returning in a few months for a December visit. Rebecca wanted to go but I thought we should explore some of Asia instead. Things were going so well, I reasoned, that we shouldn't risk taking the kids back just four months after moving to Beijing, possibly making them homesick. But now there was no doubt; we would be returning to the United States for the holidays.

Two days after that phone call, my dad had his "little surgery" to remove the tumor. The operation occurred in the middle of the night China time. I called my brother as soon as I woke up and learned that Dad had recovered, only to have some complications and have to go back under the knife. I went off to coach Jacob's soccer team, waiting anxiously for another call, which came midgame as I was sprinting up and down the pitch, simultaneously coaching and refereeing.

I took the call, pulled over to the sideline, and waved my hand around, vaguely hoping someone else would take over. The news was good. Dad was awake, responsive, and feeling fine. By the end of the week they would know whether the tumor had metastasized into the bladder, necessitating further surgery, or out of the bladder, meaning there was effectively no treatment to be had.

Three days later, I escorted my visiting in-laws to the Summer Palace, a massive park of gardens, royal residences, and lakes. We were walking down the Long Corridor, where the empress once strolled, when my dad called. I ducked away and strolled aimlessly, hearing a pinch in my own voice as I explained where I was. I barely heard him describing an upcoming gig for the Dixieland band that had earned him the nickname Dixie Doc. We both knew he wasn't calling to chat, and I was certain that this delay in getting to the point was not a good sign.

He said he had some results. The tumor hadn't spread beyond the bladder, which was good, but it was in the bladder walls, which was bad. The whole organ would have to be removed. I asked logical questions about treatment options and likely outcomes, and he remained calm and clinical, as if we were talking about someone else. I barely heard the answers.

I leaned against a railing, looking out over Kunming Lake and the famous bridge that bisects it. Thousands of Chinese tourists moved behind me, massive lines following umbrella-wielding tour guides. My in-laws were back there somewhere, but I had lost interest in the place.

The last thing I remember Dixie saying was, "Don't worry about me. I'll be fine. Don't let it ruin your time over there."

I silently rejoined my small group, walking through the grounds with my mind half a world away. I felt like a fool, numbly strolling along as our tour guide chattered away, but I didn't want to pull the plug on my visitors' day and I was not ready to discuss this quite yet. Hal and Ruth asked if everything was okay and I muttered, "Yes."

After lunch in a beautiful restaurant and a visit to the Fragrant Hills, a hillside teeming with Chinese tourists viewing the famous "red leaves" of fall, I finally told my in-laws the truth. We were speeding home in the backseat of a car driven by Mrs. Lu, one-half of a husband/wife team of drivers we had recently found. She was weaving in and out of traffic on the Fifth Ring Road, one of the broad highways that surround the city, making all of us cringe until my news caused everyone to lose track of the outside world.

A short, stunned silence set in before Hal, who is also a physician, began asking thorough medical questions, which I answered as best as I could.

"Your dad's a strong man," he finally said. "He can overcome this."

We both knew he was right about point one and just hoping about point two. My father had been ridiculously healthy and fit for most of his life, running six miles five days a week for decades. In the five years since he retired, however, he had his hip replaced, a cancerous prostate removed, and major back surgery. He had survived each of these operations remarkably well and still looked ten years younger than he was, with a full head of brown hair. Now his body would have to overcome one more indignity.

Over the next few days I was more deeply affected than I anticipated. Morbid thoughts ran through my head. Though the prognosis was pretty good, I couldn't stop pondering the worst-case scenario: that my father was dying. Pessimism, grief—even panic—flooded me, no matter how much I tried to remain rational. Among other concerns, I wondered what this would mean for our China venture. Could we stay if things didn't go well? Would we want to?

The romanticism of being on the other side of the world vanished in an instant. All the possibilities it opened up paled in comparison to the pain of being so far away during what could turn into a protracted illness. I also felt a spreading fear that he might not make it. It was hard to contemplate returning to American life without my father.

After just two months, it was obvious that he had been right when he said we couldn't say no to Beijing. I already sensed that this decision would indeed mark a turning point in our lives. Now, his illness had thrown me off stride. A couple of weeks later, he turned seventy and I felt our distance keenly, posting a tribute on my blog that had the melodramatic tone of a eulogy. I wrote:

My father Richard Paul, aka Dixie Doc, turns 70 today. Roasting Dixie is like shooting fish in a barrel. The hardest part is deciding where to start.

It could be with him stripping down in the parking lot of a Florida diner packed with senior citizens enjoying early bird dinner to sprint naked into the Gulf of Mexico. Or promoting his newly released CD while on the witness stand in a highly charged suit against Blue Cross. Or playing a show 24 hours after leaving the hospital following a major operation. That was the same surgery where he used a marker to write on his stomach before going under: "No interns. No medical students. No Foley catheter."

Happy Birthday, Dixie. Please remember that George Bernard Shaw was right when he said, "A man of great common sense and good taste—meaning thereby a man without originality or moral courage." And he was wrong when he said, "Hell is full of musical amateurs." Just don't ask Mom about the latter.

MY FELLOW MANDARIN classmate Tom Davis and I regularly discussed my fears about my father's health. He was patient, caring, and supportive—everything you would want from a friend. He never shared with me that he had his own familial health concerns; he was growing increasingly worried about his wife, Cathy.

She was experiencing mysterious and persistent back pain, which I only learned about when Theo Yardley hitched a ride to class and inquired about Cathy's health. Somehow, she knew about this problem despite rarely speaking to Tom, while I knew nothing despite seeing him several times a week. The ladies of Riviera knew what was going on in one another's lives.

"She's not doing well," Tom said, "and we can't figure out what the problem is."

I listened intently, feeling terribly self-centered about all the time Tom and I had spent talking about my father.

A dedicated athlete, Cathy had started having back pain on her regular runs. It didn't go away after repeated rests, so she visited a doctor at the Western-style, expat-oriented hospital, who diagnosed joint inflammation. But she wasn't responding to treatment, and they still had not discovered the source of the problem.

They came over for dinner one night, and the four of us ate while the kids watched a movie together in our den. Eli watched in awe as Sudha removed her legs and scooted around the floor. He ran to my side. "That girl has plastic legs!" he exclaimed.

I looked at Tom and Cathy, embarrassed. But they were unbothered. "Yes, she does," Tom said.

This was only the second or third time I had met Cathy and she seemed fine—but appearances can be deceiving. Over the next few weeks, Tom became more and more preoccupied with Cathy's health, as she kept feeling worse despite a string of negative test results. Clearly something was being missed, and an increasingly concerned Tom pushed her to return for an American checkup.

The night she left for Seattle, Tom and his girls came over

for pizza. He brought a pair of electric clippers and shaved my head as part of an ongoing show of support for my father, who was about to start his chemo. My blog became a festival of bald-headed photos as a dozen friends and family members were shorn.

I spent the next day with Tom as he waited for news. We were in the back of his van, heading home, when Cathy called. Watching his face as he offered quiet words of comfort, I braced for bad news, but still gasped when he hung up and told me with a quivering voice that Cathy was riddled with cancer.

Imaging showed that her lungs were filled with spots; she had a huge tumor on her spine, which had been the source of her original back pain; and there were indications that her cancer had spread throughout her organs. Cathy had advanced small-cell lung cancer, and there was no cure. The illness does, however, respond to aggressive chemotherapy and an earlier diagnosis would have improved her odds of living longer.

You have to undergo a thorough medical screening as part of receiving a long-term Chinese visa, including a chest x-ray. Cathy had hers while on a look-see visit to China. I had actually been annoyed that we had not known about this option on our own visit because it allowed you to do everything—blood test, EKG, chest x-ray—in one place. We had spent a whole day going to different doctors' offices to take care of this back home.

It now seemed clear that nobody had really read Cathy's x-ray; if they had, the disease would have been detected and Tom and Cathy never would have moved. Once arrived, they were at the mercy of her employer and available medical care. By the time it became obvious that she needed immediate and dramatic help—help in America—it was too late.

One of the things I liked best about Tom and Cathy was

their wholehearted embrace of China and the expat life. While others seemed to seek out things to complain about, from the speed of Internet connections to the cleanliness of public toilets, Tom and Cathy enjoyed every minute of their adventure. It was one of the things that drew us together.

But having moved to China a couple of months before her illness took hold put Tom in an extra perilous situation, as he was now homeless and jobless while facing the possibility of becoming a far-too-young widower and single father of two. It seemed particularly cruel that the new life that Tom and Cathy had embraced was making a horrible situation worse.

Tom quickly made plans to return home with the girls, and I kept him company as he packed a few bags. A Christmas tree hung with ornaments Tom and Cathy had picked up over the course of their eighteen-year relationship sat in the corner. The next day, I stopped by again to hug my friend good-bye and give the girls meager gifts of Skittles and coloring books.

While grieving over Tom's news and fretting over my father's health, I received some unexpected good news. I had edited three of my favorite blog posts filled with excitement and fascination about my new life and submitted them to the editor of WSJ.com. I quickly received an e-mail letter of acceptance, with word that the columns would be debuting in just a few weeks.

The sense of possibility and reinvention I felt from my earliest days writing blog posts about my arrival in China was paying off. But I struggled to make sense of receiving such good news while feeling so much dread for Cathy and my father.

Days later, I attended Jacob and Eli's end-of-term holiday show, an ambitious performance held in a giant tent on the soccer pitch behind their school, just outside the Riv's gates. We walked there on a cold night, feeling the chill, dry Siberian winds whip through us. The smell of coal smoke hung heavy in the air, as it did throughout the Beijing winter.

Inside the tent, warmed up by an army of towering ceramic heaters, I looked around and was overcome with emotion. I felt a surge of pride for my whole family. This felt like a graduation ceremony for our first semester in China, and we had all passed with flying colors. The new column was gravy, but thinking about my good fortune made me ponder my friends' predicament and how fast their lives had been turned upside down.

Tears streamed down my cheeks as I thought about Tom and Cathy. No one noticed in the dark tent, but I grabbed Becky's hand and squeezed it hard. For all the adventures and experiences we had already had in China, nothing topped the simple, profound joy of watching our kids in an elementary school play. I felt certain that Cathy would never experience this and terribly guilty about thinking about her in the past tense. I had a deep sense of doom.

A WEEK LATER, I was sitting in my parents' den in Pittsburgh, with Rebecca and our kids. My father was half asleep on the couch, struggling to stay awake as my kids watched *Dumbo* and wrestled on the floor, their pent-up energy the result of too much time spent indoors.

I accompanied my father, who was a shadow of his normal self, to a chemo session. It was humbling to observe cancer's equal-opportunity hunger, with patients of every age, color, ethnicity, and income level sitting side by side receiving IV drips.

My column debuted while we were visiting, and my father told me how proud he was. He had become much more open in talking about his feelings after his first bout with cancer, and now he was throwing around "I love you's" like confetti at a parade.

When it was time to leave, there was no way to squelch the thought that I could be saying good-bye for the last time. Before leaving for the airport, he told me to go into the front closet and find his giant, forty-year-old down coat. "It kept me warm in Alaska," he said. "It should take care of those Siberian winds."

I hugged my dad and told him I'd be back in April when he had his bladder removed. He said it was too far and my responsibilities were too great; my family needed me in China.

"But my family also needs me in America," I replied. "We'll work it out and I'll be back."


EARLY IN THE spring, Tom called to say he was coming to Beijing to empty out the house. They had officially signed papers saying they weren't returning, and the company wanted the house off the books. It seemed a cold-blooded request, but I was happy to see my friend.

He tried to be optimistic, but the prognosis was grim. Doctors had given Cathy a slim chance of survival. I once again kept him company as he packed up his house, including wrapping up the ornaments on the withered Christmas tree.

The next day, my family and I left for a long-planned trip, which we had delayed to see Tom. We hugged good-bye in front of his house again.


WHILE ON THE trip I finished a close-to-the-bone column about Dixie's illness and how it affected me from so far away. I labored over every word and felt like I was publicly exposing my emotions more than I ever had, making the flood of supportive reader e-mail particularly moving. One message especially struck me, beginning with one simple line:

> Reading your column, I was frankly overcome with envy over your relationship with your father.

It took a stranger's note for me to acknowledge the obvious, that I really loved my father and greatly valued our relationship, and that the thought of him being gone was turning my world upside down.

I had decided to wait until a few days after his surgery to return; everyone else would be there for the operation, my mother said, and he would need visitors afterward. My mother promised that she would call as soon as the seven-hour operation to remove his bladder and craft a new one from his small intestines was over, no matter what time it was in Beijing.

I woke up with a start at 6:00 a.m., worried that I hadn't heard anything yet. I drank coffee and tried to read a magazine until my phone finally rang. My mother, speaking through tears, said that when she and my sister arrived in the recovery room five minutes after my father woke up, the nurse already knew her patient's name was Dixie Doc and that he played the trumpet. We both understood that this meant that although his bladder was gone, his essence was intact. She handed him the phone. Though his voice was reduced to a hoarse whisper, he sounded very much alive.

It was the end of a long, emotionally grueling day in New York, but early in the morning in Beijing. I felt like I could fully relax for the first time in months. As I walked outside to take the kids to school, Theo came running up our walk, a tear trickling down her cheek.

"Cathy's dead," she blurted, before breaking into sobs.

. . . .

CATHY DIED SHORTLY after Tom returned from Beijing. He had barely made it back to his wife's bedside at her parents' home in Portland, Oregon.

Cathy's mother answered the phone, and a beat passed before I said anything. I panicked and contemplated hanging up, but willed some words out.

"This is Alan Paul calling from Beijing. I just wanted you to know that Cathy was loved and is missed here."

"Thank you," she said, with remarkable composure. "Cathy loved China."

Tom got on the phone and sounded a million miles away. I told him I was thinking of him and would do anything to help, but we both knew there was nothing I could do.

FIVE DAYS AFTER Dixie's surgery, I left my family in Beijing and boarded a plane to see my family in New York. It felt strange to leave the kids behind, and I had a nagging sense that I had lost something, constantly feeling for my wallet and making sure I had my backpack.

Aunt Joan and Uncle Ben picked me up and drove me into Manhattan, where I found my father sitting up in bed wearing an ancient pair of giant glasses. He looked old and tired but far better than I had anticipated. I gave him a hug.

The next morning, he was talking about checking himself out of the hospital and returning to Pittsburgh. It seemed like a bad idea, but nearly fifty years as a doctor had taught him one thing, he said: "Hospitals are a good place to die and a great place to get out of as soon as possible." I saw him check himself out against doctor's orders a few years earlier after a hip replacement, so I shouldn't have been surprised.

Two days later, my father and I were strolling through the Pittsburgh neighborhood where I grew up. He walked gingerly—no surprise given that he was wearing a catheter—but was remarkably steady on his feet.

The Pirates were playing the Dodgers the next afternoon, and he surprised me by suggesting that we "go down to the stadium, have a pulled pork sandwich for lunch, and watch the game for a while."

My mom dropped us at the door of PNC Park, we bought scalped box seats for twenty dollars and were sitting in the sun by the top of the second inning. The pulled pork was on the other side of the stadium so I ate a Pittsburgh-famous Primanti's sandwich, while Dixie munched on some chicken wings. Few meals have ever been so satisfying.

He thanked me for coming all the way from Beijing and sounded optimistic that he would have a good recovery, but he didn't want to talk too much about how he was feeling. Being there together was enough. I had expected to spend a week sitting by a New York hospital bed.

Two days later, I returned to Beijing, amazed at Dixie's resilience. When I collapsed into my seat for the return flight, I felt relieved that my father seemed to be firmly on the road to recovery. But for the first time in a week I also began to reflect on Tom and Cathy and felt a crushing sadness. I missed Becky and the kids terribly and couldn't wait to get back to them. Home was wherever they were—wherever *we* were—and I understood that with a new clarity.

# CHAPTER 10

# NO PARTICULAR PLACE TO GO

We took to the roads as soon as we got our licenses, and I enjoyed piloting that rickety old Beijing Jeep with its booming V-8 engine. I felt hardcore and macho driving it, with every liver-rattling bump reaffirming that I was on a rugged, wild adventure. I started going regularly to the Sunhe Market, a run-down, sprawling place up the street from our house, on the side of Jing Shun Lu.

It was widely known as the Kite Market, because of the huge, brightly covered kites that individual vendors sold in front. It was a dusty, dirty place with a parking lot filled with craterlike potholes and ringed by vendors selling produce, "antique" knickknacks, and cooked food like scallion pancakes and noodles.

Anchoring the market was an outlet of the Wu Mei convenience store chain, a bizarre bazaar stocked with such staples as rice cookers, blouses, chili peppers, grain alcohol, and cigarettes. I once inexplicably found Pabst Blue Ribbon there—I never saw it again in China—and bought two six-packs. But the market's real heart was next door in a huge warehouse-like building, which housed everything from produce to hardware, butcher shops to DVDs.

One time I took my Chinese teacher Yechen with me to help negotiate a price to repair an old TV. He always warned me to be careful, worried that Chinese merchants viewed foreigners as little more than walking ATMs. In the back corner of a back building, we found a small electronics repair booth. As we waited for the repairman to return from lunch, we chatted with his wife and a couple of her friends. They had never met anyone quite like the educated, erudite Yechen and were shocked that he could speak English. Listening to us talk, they didn't believe he was Chinese, repeatedly asking whether he was Japanese or Korean.

Yechen laughed and insisted he was Han—an ethnic Chinese. Finally believing him, they pointed at me.

"Look how big and strong the American is compared to us," one said. I probably outweighed my slight teacher by fifty pounds. "That's because we only eat rice, and they eat meat and butter every meal."

The opportunity for such interactions was a big part of the reason I loved shopping there, even though one friend's driver so disliked the filthy place that she finally asked her employer why she insisted on returning to the market. "Even we won't shop here, so why do you?" she asked.

We liked it because it was fun, and the adventure started long before the shopping even began. I loved bouncing my Jeep across the wrecked parking lot, but I knew that pretending I was a frontiersman didn't make much sense.

Back home, we had purchased two minivans based on federal safety tests and obsessed about buying proper car seats for our children. Now we were piling them into the back of a thirteen-year-old car that seemed likely to drop into three sections if it was rear-ended and that had backseat seat belts that barely worked. This was in line with the fact that our safety standards had plummeted with amazing speed immediately upon arriving in China.

When we went downtown on our very first weekend, Kathy Chen called us a car service, but the five of us piled into a seat-belt-less taxi to head home. We handed the driver a printed business card with our compound's address, just hoping he would get us back from Fundazzle.

I crawled into the front seat, folded myself into a cage-like device, and felt guilty buckling my seat belt; Becky was crammed into the small backseat with three kids and no restraints. Jacob was staring out the window, watching Beijing go by, but Eli was flopping around the floor, and Anna was scrambling toward the gearshift and reaching for me. Becky and I were trying to corral the kids and force them to sit back and stay still while the driver yelled at us, not because he was worried about a kid flying through the windshield but because they were putting their dirty feet all over his seat's cloth covering.

We were behaving as if living in China protected us with a cosmic force field, but the opposite was actually true; the road fatality rate there is freakishly high. That was little more than a passing thought until one night when I was driving home, down Jing Shun Lu, with all three kids jammed into the backseat. Rebecca was not with me so I had no way to control the kids fighting in the back as I maneuvered the treacherous road. Unsecured by the floppy seat belt, Anna's car seat was swinging around, toppling onto Eli, who screamed and pushed the seat flying onto Jacob on the other side. They were all yelling at me and at one another.

We were surrounded by trucks, most of them carrying

massively overloaded payloads extending off every side of their beds, without any flags or markers. This was a typical night. Large trucks were banned from driving in the city's core until 10:00 p.m. As the hour drew near, trucks flooded down from the north, making an always tough drive terrifying. When we finally got home, I told Becky that we had to buy a new car.

She agreed, and we both assumed that a few weeks later we'd be driving a new vehicle. We began searching for a minivan with seven seats and two airbags. It says a lot about how cushy expat packages can be that most of our friends were surprised that we had to shop for and purchase our own vehicle.

A couple of people told me they purchased cars with the help of "Beijing Bob," who was said to make the process quick and painless. After browsing his website, I told him we were interested in one of a confusing array of Chinese vans that had something do with Mitsubishi and were all grouped together on his site, mysteriously ranging in price from about $14,000 to $24,000. He said he would arrange for us to see them. Bob spoke English with a heavy accent and I assumed he was Chinese, but eventually I learned that he is actually an expat from Sierra Leone, Africa, who favors shiny suits.

The next day, Bob's employee "Alice" called and said she could take us to see Mitsubishi and also vans "with Mitsubishi engines" at the same dealer. The place was "close, close," she said. "Just off the Fourth Ring Road." The Fourth Ring Road ran close to our house, but it circles Beijing and once Alice's driver got on it, we turned south and drove nearly to the other side of the city, passing at least two Mitsubishi dealers en route. When I asked Alice, who was Chinese, about this, she pretended not to understand me.

After forty minutes, we exited the main road and drove

through a maze of side streets before emerging near a string of car dealers. Rather than pulling into one of them, however, we parked by the side of a dirt field bisected by a metal construction fence. Rebecca was coming from the office and she called to say Mr. Dou was lost, giving both of us pause; he never got lost. Alice's driver took the phone, and he and Mr. Dou had a discussion that grew so animated I thought they would brawl when they met. I hadn't realized yet that this is a common conversational mode for two Chinese men.

A young woman appeared, peeling back a section of the fence to allow us through. We crossed the rutted dirt field and entered a large, unmarked hangar. Four vans sat in the middle, covered with a heavy layer of dust and grime. Alice cheerfully said, "Here they are." The dusty cars represented the different models, from cheapest (manual transmission, cloth seats, no air bags) to most expensive (leather seats, dual airbags, DVD player).

By the time Becky arrived, it had started raining. I walked back out to meet her at the fence and we exchanged a look that mixed humor and alarm as we crossed the increasingly muddy, rutted field. We asked Alice if we could take the top-of-the-line model for a test drive. Everyone seemed puzzled by this, but then agreed. We drove a 15-mph loop on the bumpy dirt road around the large building. The car seemed okay, and Mr. Dou approved, but I had serious reservations about the distracting in-dash DVD player, which could not be turned off while a movie was watched in the back.

I also could not understand what made this car, which bore a Chinese logo, a Mitsubishi. "Mitsubishi engine," Alice explained.

"What about this one?" I pointed to the slightly cheaper model.

"Mitsubishi design."

. . . .

A FEW DAYS later, I set out to buy a car by myself, driving to a Mitsubishi dealer near my home that I had seen from the highway. I inquired about a van, only to be told *"mei you"* (don't have any). Maybe there was a "Mitsubishi design" or "Mitsubishi engine" showroom somewhere in Beijing.

The salesman signaled to wait, then disappeared. A moment later, another guy emerged. He spoke English haltingly and with great effort, though he seemed to understand everything. He explained that his name was Mr. Liu and he had his own company, Expat Cars, to assist people like me.

A few days later, we canvassed the city, looking at Volkswagens (too small), Buicks (too expensive—almost $50,000), and Kias (surprisingly too expensive) before ending up at another "Mitsubishi-designed" dealer, where the vans were housed inside a nicely lit building. They even had the option of leather seats and automatic transmission without that insane DVD player.

The dealer was asking 168,000 renminbi, or $24,000. I was suspicious that Mr. Liu couldn't get them to budge; this is a country where you haggle to the death over one-dollar socks. Mr. Dou visited the dealer and could only move them 300 RMB, so we knew we had a fair deal.

Now we just had to figure out how to get the dealer all that money, because financing was not an option. I wired the funds into my Chinese account and converted it from dollars, which took several visits. When I had enough money in the account, I asked for a cashier's check; the manager looked at me as if I had inquired if she laid eggs. They don't do checks in China, so I could either transfer the money into the dealer's account, or withdraw bags of 100 RMB notes, as most Chinese customers do.

I opted for the wire and two days later, Mr. Liu drove our new van to the house, complete with license plates and proof of insurance. It had been months since we decided to make the purchase. We drove downtown to meet one of Rebecca's reporters. "Nice car," he said. "What is it?"

I smiled. "Mitsubishi engine and design."

# CHAPTER 11

# LONESOME AND A LONG
# WAY FROM HOME

Returning to Maplewood after one year in China reminded me of the feeling I had leaving the hospital after our first child was born. Everything had a brighter, more intense focus and I sensed that nothing would ever look quite the same again.

On a family stroll into town, the tree-lined streets became objects of fascination. We marveled at sights that were common in leafy, suburban America but seemed wondrous coming from dusty, dry Beijing: chirping birds and scampering squirrels, a cool, gentle breeze and morning light filtering through the dense overhead foliage.

I was looking at everything with new eyes, making the familiar suddenly look foreign. Something had changed within me, and I was trying to sort out exactly what it meant. Within a few days, though, everything began to look normal again. It started to feel like I had never left, as if the whole year had just been a vivid dream. This was both comforting and disturbing.

As the weeks rolled by, we made pilgrimages to Beach Haven, New Jersey; Pittsburgh, Pennsylvania; and Bay City,

Michigan. Visiting these familiar, favorite places and the friends and family in each of them was comforting, but the cumulative effect of dragging kids and bags from place to place for a month was quite the opposite.

I started to feel lost in time and space, not quite on vacation but definitely not home. Eventually, I felt strangely disassociated from everything; I was neither here nor there. I was longing for Beijing and wondering just what, exactly, I wanted to get back to. I missed my house and possessions—the things you see every day that ground you and remind you who you are—but it was deeper than that. When I unexpectedly heard an elderly Chinese couple speaking Mandarin in a park in Bay City, I felt like hugging them. Instead, I just said *"ni hao"* (hello) and engaged in some light chitchat. It fueled my desire to get back to Beijing. We were ready to get back to our lives. We were ready to go home.

When Rebecca and Anna returned to Beijing so she could get back to work, I stayed in Maplewood with the boys for another week. It was a plan that made sense when we were booking flights months earlier, but that now felt like a mistake. I wasn't surprised to not enjoy the family separation, but I was shocked to sit in Maplewood feeling so homesick for Beijing.

I tried to relax and make the most of my extra week, getting together with friends for two freewheeling basement jam sessions that reactivated my musical passion. I bought a new guitar to stay motivated, a beautiful Epiphone 335, with a big, fat body and a vibrant sunburst finish. After all those musical near misses, I was determined to make something happen.

At the airport, I detuned the strings to reduce tension on the neck and checked the guitar, secure in its hardshell case. Then I boarded the plane with my boys, somewhat apprehensive about flying solo, but relieved to not have Anna with me. Her calling card was falling asleep shortly after boarding, taking a catnap, being brutally awake for the entire flight, and falling back to sleep on descent. She was still too young to be distracted by electronics for long, so we would read, draw, patrol the aisles, and play with the Chinese kids who were always traveling with their grandparents to or from a visit to their parents.

Still, I knew there would be rough moments. There always were. People sometimes asked for advice about how to handle long flights with kids, as if I had become a guru. But the only tangible thing that experience provided was the knowledge that you will eventually, somehow, make it alive to the other side of the world.

That seemingly obvious point becomes invaluable to remember when things are at their bleakest—when you are somewhere over the Arctic Circle, seven or eight hours from landing and contemplating whether or not it's possible to unscrew your head and place it in the carry-on compartment.

On each of these endless flights I had reached a point where I swore that I just couldn't make it—usually about halfway through, when we had eaten a couple of meals and assisted the kids in reading, drawing, playing their Game Boys, and watching two movies, only to realize that we had seven hours to go, I was bone tired, the kids simply would not sleep, and every battery was dead. Then I would somehow do the impossible and get the kids to sleep, often with Jacob spreading out on the floor, against all FAA regulations. By the time we got up, descent would be imminent, light illuminating the end of a very long tunnel. And so it was this time. Fifteen hours after boarding, we landed in Beijing.

I was happy to see Mr. Dou waiting for us. Everything looked grayer and dustier than I remembered, but it felt good to be back and I smiled when we turned on to the crazy Jing Shun Lu. We inched up the road, wedged in between buses, with electric bikes zipping by on each side of us, past the guy selling giant vases and clay pots on the side of the road. It all looked at once exotic and utterly familiar, and I saw the boys were also peering out the window, anxious to turn into the Riv.

When we got home, Jacob and Eli jumped out of the car and immediately joined friends playing in the street. With Becky at work and Anna off with Ding Ayi, I carried my new guitar up to my office, eager to tune up and play a few "welcome to Beijing" licks.

I opened the case and recoiled at the gruesome sight in front of me: the headstock was dangling off the neck, held on only by loose, flapping strings. I placed the instrument back in its case, which I closed and shoved under my desk.

# CHAPTER 12

# CAN'T LOSE WHAT YOU NEVER HAD

With both of our fortieth birthdays approaching, Rebecca and I planned a big bash at the Orchard featuring a great African band. I marked my actual birthday by joining a weekly hike led by a friend. We drove two hours northwest of the city, up and over a tall, twisty mountain pass and down into the countryside, arriving in a little village filled with elderly people. Virtually every resident under fifty had left for the city.

Our driver went off in search of the local party leader to hire a guide, returning with a tiny, gnarled man who looked seventy-five but said he was fifty-two. Just outside the village we came upon a beautiful old temple. Unlike many similar places, it had survived both Japanese occupation in the 1930s and 1940s and the Cultural Revolution of the 1960s and 1970s. Our guide, who smoked constantly, said it had not been an active temple since his childhood, but the center building still contained faded Buddha statues. A back room stored coffins, including several large, decorative caskets festively painted bright red and orange. They were used for elderly people, he said, "happy funerals," marking the end of a long life.

We bushwhacked our way up a ridge, passing donkeys grazing on the end of long leashes and old men and women tending their crabapple trees. At the top, we sat down for lunch before heading down, with the guide beating the shoulder-high grass with a large stick—to scare off the many snakes, he explained. We walked down the other side of the mountain where we followed a twisty country road into a tiny village. We visited the crumbling courtyard home of an old woman whom the hikers had met on an earlier trip, bought handwoven straw baskets and walnuts from villagers, and headed for the only shop in town.

Entering the general store was like stepping into 1963, with a faded poster of Mao overlooking the merchandise from a back wall. The store sold everything from hoses and rakes to giant bags of rice and cans of cooking oil. They also had cold beer—never a given in China, especially in rural areas, because of the cost of refrigeration—and I bought a twenty-ounce Tsingtao for a quarter and took a welcome, refreshing swig. Two others in my group also bought beers, and we clinked bottles as I silently wished myself a happy birthday.

Many people had been asking if I was struggling with the big birthday, wondering if I was feeling depressed or concerned about getting old. These questions were starting to bug me because I kept thinking about Cathy Davis, who was thirty-nine when she died and would have given anything to see her fortieth birthday. It would insult her memory to view getting older as anything other than a gift, or to take a single moment for granted. I was especially committed to taking full advantage of every day we had in China, even if doing so required a complete reassessment of our routines.

As we began our second year in Beijing, our primary challenges had shifted 180 degrees, from establishing normalcy to battling complacency. Our weekends largely revolved around the same things they do for countless suburban American families—kids' soccer and baseball games, Sunday school and birthday parties, dinner in friends' backyards and occasional nights out on the town. I didn't want life to become *too* normal. We were Americans living in China for a few brief years. Should status quo suburban living really be our goal?

With China beckoning, we needed to strike a balance between a nice, stable existence and taking full advantage of this unique chapter in our lives. Soccer games and birthday parties would be around for years to come, while the Great Wall, the terracotta warriors, and Beijing's labyrinthine, ancient hutong neighborhoods would not—at least for us. A new year was starting, and I had an acute understanding of just how fast it could pass. I heard a clock faintly ticking in the background every day and was determined to make the most of my time in China.

When Kathy Chen and her family returned to the United States, we hired Hou Ayi, their longtime employee, and an incredibly warmhearted, efficient woman who was a tremendous cook. A former accountant who would probably be running a corporation if she had been born two decades later, she operated in the kitchen like a Swiss clock. She shopped with similar precision, rooting through a pile of scallions in search of the perfect one, and I loved going to the market with her and watching her shop and haggle.

Kathy had helped Hou Ayi learn many Western dishes, translating from American cookbooks into Chinese, but we told her to stick mostly with Chinese cooking. We enjoyed eating it every day. And when I really wanted a taste of America I visited one of several restaurants or fired up my barbecue and grilled meat purchased at the excellent German butcher.

. . . .

AT ONE NEIGHBORHOOD gathering, I spent much of the night speaking to my American neighbors Dave and Katherine Loevinger, as gangs of kids ran around playing with one another. Dave was the U.S. Treasury Department representative in Beijing, deeply respected in the economics community, but we were talking about music. He had spent years playing saxophone with a popular Washington R&B band.

I invited Dave and Katherine to our birthday party the next week and told him to bring his sax. I had no idea how good he was, but he seemed to know his stuff and I had never played with a saxophonist. It sounded like fun.

With my new guitar broken, I took my old Fender Stratocaster over to the Orchard and checked in with the band, which featured two Africans, an American keyboardist, and three Chinese who could nail the beats perfectly. I wanted to sit in for a few tunes and lead them for one—Bob Dylan's "You're Gonna Make Me Lonesome When You Go," the only song I felt comfortable singing in public. We ran through it once before I went out to greet arriving guests.

A few hours later, with the party in full swing, I joined the band, kicked off the song's three-chord opening, made sure everyone fell in, and started singing. Surrounded by friends, I felt surprisingly comfortable. I saw Dave over by the side, adjusting his reed, fiddling with his sax and looking tentative. As I began the second verse, I nodded, silently inviting him to join. He walked up to a mic and played a couple of tasty fills.

As I finished the final verse I signaled him to solo, and he began blasting out a soulful statement that lifted and launched the entire group to a new level. Nothing focuses a band like an inspired soloist, and Dave was fantastic, putting himself into every dynamic note. I dug into my Strat, putting my all into the rhythm as I felt my heart beat faster. Every lick he played made me happier and more confident.

A few weeks later, I was invited to perform with one of Beijing's top jazz bands. I would be in over my head, but the evening was part of Danny Pearl World Music Night, an international celebration of the *Wall Street Journal* reporter who was slain in Pakistan shortly after 9/11. I was being invited in part because I was a *WSJ* columnist. I didn't want to say no but was scared as soon as I said yes.

I asked Dave to come along, feeling much more confident knowing he would be by my side. We took the stage together, and I led the group through three blues numbers. Learning Chinese had liberated me enough that singing in public no longer terrified me, and the positive feedback when I walked offstage was a thrill. The owner of the club, camped out in back with a big cigar and a tray of green tea, raised a toast to me and gave me a thumbs-up. "Very good," he said.

Now I wanted more. I wanted to play with Dave again. I wanted to figure out a way to jam regularly. And I wanted my broken guitar back. My gear gurus at *Guitar World* assured me the problem was completely fixable—if I could find a competent repairman in Beijing.

# CHAPTER 13

# CAST OFF ALL MY FEARS

Feeling a new urgency to get my guitar fixed, I sent out an e-mail query to a few friends and received two replies with the same advice: Woodie Wu could help me. The young Chinese guitarist was just back from a three-year stint in Australia, fluent in English and running Purple Buzz, a guitar repair shop and music management company.

I had always been hesitant to mention my *Guitar World* affiliation when dealing with guitar shops. It felt pompous and name-droppy and led salesmen to launch into one-upmanship. But this was different; I was in China and wanted to make sure that I got good service from the guy with the cool name.

Dear Woodie. This is Alan Paul from Guitar World magazine. I am in Beijing with a broken Epi 335. I've been told that you can fix it. Let me know if I can bring my guitar down for you to look at.

His reply came quickly:

> I looked you up online. You have interviewed many of my
> idols. I would be happy to fix your guitar.

Woodie and I set a date for me to bring him both the guitar and my long-busted amp. Mrs. Lu drove into the large gray Maoist apartment complex filled with identical, bland brick structures where his office was located. Woodie directed her to his building and said he'd meet me at the door. He appeared as I got out of the car wrestling with the gear.

The perfect picture of a Chinese rocker, Woodie was wearing ripped jeans and a worn jean jacket over a faded Beatles T-shirt, with long black hair obscuring his face. A wallet chain rode around his right hip, Tibetan turquoise glistened around his neck, and his feet were clad in scuffed black Doc Martens boots. Woodie smiled and extended his hand to shake—not always a given in meeting a Chinese friend. He grabbed the amp out of my hand and motioned for me to follow him up the dingy staircase to his office.

In a back workshop, Woodie introduced me to "Eric," the thin, bespectacled repairman who worked for him. We took the Epiphone out of its case and Eric carefully studied it, a cigarette dangling between his lanky fingers. He turned it over, eyed the cracked headstock, then looked up and spoke rapidly to Woodie in Chinese.

"He says he can fix it," Woodie told me. "It will take some time but be as good as new."

Anxious to hear some tales about my years at *Guitar World*, Woodie invited me into the outer office to have a Coke. Sitting together at a little table, we talked about my interactions with some of the guitarists he revered and about some of the shows I had seen over the years. But I was more interested in quizzing him about the Beijing music scene, which I had barely begun to explore. I didn't know what kind of music Woodie himself liked or played until I saw the unmistakable face of Stevie Ray Vaughan peeking out from under his left sleeve. I had never been more surprised or excited to see a tattoo.

Woodie's arms were covered with tribal tats, but that distinct image belonged to the American blues guitar great whose presence had loomed large over my *Guitar World* career. I couldn't believe that I had found a Chinese guy with an SRV tattoo. Woodie couldn't believe that an American *Guitar World* editor who had been intimately involved in archival Vaughan CDs—I had written lengthy essays for two prominent releases—had walked into his Beijing office.

Our talk turned to blues and I got my second pleasant surprise when Woodie, twenty-nine, told me that after a decade of playing lead guitar, he was now focusing on harmonica and lap steel guitar. Lap steel is a form of electric slide guitar, a sound for which I have always had a deep affinity—it is at the core of the Allman Brothers music, which captivated me so long ago and continued to cast a spell.

We talked about seeing some bands together and getting together for a jam, and I headed home dizzy with the possibilities of not only getting my guitar back but maybe having something really fun to do with it.

Woodie and I e-mailed regularly for six weeks, then I received this e-mail:

> Guitar is ready. I am playing with a band called Sand Friday night. Do you want to come pick it up there?

WOODIE WAS SITTING with his bandmates in a booth in the back of the Get Lucky Club sharing large bottles of Tsingtao.

He rose to greet me and apologetically said they were having a band meeting. "The guitar is right over there." He nodded toward the stage. "Have a look."

I opened the case and picked up the guitar, which seemed as good as new. As I played it, Woodie walked over. "Looks good, right? Want to try it out tonight with a little jam?"

"Sure."

There was a bill in the case, underneath the guitar, but Woodie did not mention it or seem in any hurry to get paid. This stood out in a culture where everyone generally fears getting ripped off and payment is always expected up front.

In the middle of a swirly Pink Floyd–styled blues song, which Woodie was bringing alive with atmospheric slide guitar textures and overtones, bandleader Liu Donghong motioned me to the stage. I plugged in, adding some concise fills and playing a short, decent solo. I remained in the background for one more song and thought I heard Woodie say they'd call me back later as I walked off.

I watched alone from a front table, nearly choking on a sip of beer when Liu suddenly said my name, pointed at me, and walked away clapping. He was turning the band over to me. I made my way onto the stage, which suddenly looked very large. As I adjusted my guitar, I looked out into the house and saw the eyes of the small Chinese crowd squarely upon me. I glanced at Woodie, hoping for a suggestion, but, like the rest of the band, he was impassively waiting for me to call a song.

I rifled my brain for something I could sing with a simple, repetitive chord structure and started strumming the Rolling Stones' "Dead Flowers," a country-tinged song ready-made for lap steel. As the band fell in, I leaned into the song's vocals just enough to wobble off the ground and take tentative flight.

The rhythm section was digging in, the lead guitarist was

playing fills behind me on his white Strat, and as I finished the second chorus, I nodded at Woodie, who played a pitch-perfect, well-constructed solo. As soon as he took off, I felt exactly as I had the first time I played with Dave: inspired. We brought the song down for a surprisingly smooth landing, and everyone looked to me again.

I yelled out "E!" and dug into the hard-charging country swing rhythm of "Deep Elem Blues," a traditional acoustic blues from the 1930s later popularized by the Grateful Dead. It's a fun song to play, with lots of room for wide-open solo-ing, and everyone fell in behind me. When the band urged one more song, I launched into a simplified version of the Allman Brothers' "Southbound." Afterward, the guitarist and bassist came over to shake hands, and Woodie and I drank beers and promised to stay in touch.

OVER THE NEXT few days, I kept hearing a sound in my head with Woodie's slide guitar in one ear and Dave's sax in the other, and my own guitar and voice in the middle. I wasn't sure it made a lot of sense, but I had stumbled onto two dynamic musicians who were interested in playing with me. I had to see where I could take this.

I half expected Woodie to make up excuses to not get together, so I was relieved when he quickly responded to my e-mailed band suggestion.

I really enjoyed your singing and playing and would be very interested in playing together. The saxophone sounds like a great idea. I will find bass and drums.

With that long-discussed Orchard open mic offer on the

table, I suggested we start out as an acoustic duo and see how it went. Woodie and I met up in a tiny basement studio down-town for two hours, running through Bob Dylan, Grateful Dead, and blues songs—the choices dictated simply by what I could sing somewhat comfortably. It went well and I set up a date at the Orchard, in just three weeks.

Needing a name right away, I made a list of my favorite blues songs and performers, hoping something would click. Then I wrote down our names, searching for a play on words, and there it was: *Woodie Alan*. How could I not use that? A smile crossed my lips and a thought flashed through my mind: we were fated to do this.

I compiled an e-mail list of fifty names and sent out an invitation:

Hello Beijing friends.

I am performing at the Orchard next Saturday. I have a great musical partner, the wonderfully named Woodie Wu. We had no choice but to call ourselves Woodie Alan.

We'll start around 7 pm and play some blues, some Dylan, and anything else we can remember. It should be fun.

It is our first performance, so please make sure to have a few drinks with dinner. It is also an open mic following our performance, with people invited to join us or take over the stage for a song or two.

So please come. Leave your rotten tomatoes at home, but bring along that mandolin, guitar, bongo or fiddle that's sitting in the back of your closet.

I hit send and almost immediately felt a surge of panic. On the basis of one rough rehearsal, I had just invited virtually everyone I knew in Beijing to watch our debut performance at one of my favorite restaurants. Why hadn't we anonymously played a few open mics downtown? We needed more rehearsal.

I asked Jonathan Ansfield, an American journalist who ran one of my favorite bars, the Stone Boat, if we could rehearse there. The Boat was a literal stone boat sitting in a lake in downtown's lovely Ritan Park. In warmer weather, bands played on a little stage extending over the water, and two patios filled with guests, but it was quiet and cozy in the winter. Without the outside seating, the Boat had just a few tables, with a small bar and a tiny kitchen in the rear. A half loft was accessible by ladder. It had bright red walls and exposed beams painted in the festive, multicolored style of old Chinese temples and palaces.

I invited Dave to join us, though I couldn't really picture a sax fitting into an acoustic duo; I imagined the group with him being an entirely different operation, but hoped we could start with a song or two. That night, in front of a handful of people, Dave wailed through the Grateful Dead's "Friend of the Devil," Bob Dylan's "Knockin' on Heaven's Door," and everything else that I thought would be too acoustic to handle a sax. Having him by my side was reassuring; I felt my panic receding.

"You guys sound great," Jonathan said, sitting down to join us. "Let me know when you want to play here."

After two rehearsals, we already had a second gig lined up. Becky was amused by this whole operation, especially my chutzpah in inviting everyone I knew to come see me perform at the Orchard. Despite her own success, she had an intense aversion to self-promotion. I probably inherited my brazen streak from my father, who was famous for inviting everyone from the mail carrier to the jurors from court to come see him perform. I had always had a sense that I could pull something like this off, and inviting so many people and promoting my music aggressively was also a form of putting pressure on myself, forcing me to really step up my game. My confidence was buoyed when playing with Dave and Woodie, and I was happy that we had one more rehearsal to polish everything.

THE SECOND REHEARSAL did not go as planned. I answered the phone in the cab to the Stone Boat and knew something was wrong as soon as I heard Dave's rough, stress-filled whisper.

"I don't think I am going to make it over," he said. "I unexpectedly have become the focal point of the Six-Party Talks."

A banking disagreement had put the Treasury Department—and Dave—in the middle of these nuclear arms negotiations with North Korea, which seemed to drag on forever and go nowhere. Hearing the ambient noise, I pictured him bent over, with his head under the table.

"Are you there now?"

"Yes. Can't talk long. If I get out earlier than expected, I will come over. Otherwise, I'll just hope I can make it Saturday night. I have been pulled into a vortex."

I had invited three friends to the rehearsal to give us an audience and some feedback and to force myself to play and sing under the eyes of people I knew. Alone with Woodie, I stumbled through "Soulshine," an anthem written by the Allman Brothers' Warren Haynes, and the Marvin Gaye classic "How Sweet It Is." We tried to work them out, but the more we broke the songs down, the worse I sounded. When one of my guests suggested that I was "missing the E minor on the 'How Sweet' vocal melody," I began to feel nauseated. I had no clue what notes I was singing. The whole episode was making me feel profoundly unstageworthy.

The debut performance at the Orchard was two days away, and humiliation seemed likely. The next morning, I followed the sage counsel of an old friend, who e-mailed a list of advice for the gig, culminating in " . . . most importantly, PRACTICE A LOT!"

Bathrooms have always been one of my favorite places to play guitar because the acoustics are great in the enclosed, tiled space. I took my guitar into our large master bath, planted myself in front of the mirror with a set list, and sang the entire planned performance, forcing myself to hold eye contact with myself.

I ran through a dozen songs, then repeatedly returned to "Soulshine" and "How Sweet It Is" until I could finally sing both steadily. I repeated this solo rehearsal the next day, just hours before taking the stage. A year later, Woodie laughed hard when I told him about this. "I had no idea you were nervous," he exclaimed. I hid it well.

Dave made it to the gig and we had a huge turnout. We were a novelty act, and this expat life offered up a ready-made, captive audience. One thing I had learned from watching my dad was that people give their friends a huge benefit of the doubt because they enjoy seeing people they know perform. I also learned to keep plowing ahead no matter what and to never apologize for yourself.

A rational approach would have been to play the songs we felt most comfortable with for forty-five minutes, but I opted to play two sets of stretched out, solo-heavy music, just like the Allman Brothers or Grateful Dead. Reaching high paid off in the long run, and it felt completely natural in our go-for-it environment.

As my friend Matt Carberry, an entrepreneur who always had an ambitious new project under way, said, "Beijing encourages you to make mistakes in all the right ways."

Wading into the crowd to find Becky after our first set, I was greeted like a conquering hero, with friends patting me on the back, buying me beers, and hoisting toasts. No one realized how much insecurity I had defeated by climbing onto that stage. My friends were having fun and accepting me as a performer. This was not being perceived as a joke. I had to relax and let it flow, which I began to do in the second set, after unplugging the monitor speaker in front of me so I no longer could hear my voice booming back at me.

More friends stopped by on their way home from other outings, and people finished eating in the back and pushed toward the stage. Encouraged by the growing crowd, we played a few songs too many, venturing onto thin ice. But I walked off the stage just before midnight swollen with pride. Dave was less impressed.

"That was a good start," he said. "When are we going to get a rhythm section?"

I was going to point out that we were developing a unique acoustic trio sound, but Woodie agreed with Dave.

"I know some people I can contact," he said.

As we sat down with friends to celebrate, Lisa's husband and business partner, Ertao Wu, joined us.

"You guys were pretty good," he said.

A musician himself, he was no doubt most impressed simply by the number of people who showed up, but that was fine. "Call Lisa about another date; let's do it again next month."

# CHAPTER 14

# LET IT GROW

I kept hearing from people who enjoyed our debut, including one Australian friend, who thanked me, saying, "I haven't seen my husband move like that in twenty years." Within a week, we had booked another gig at the Orchard and one at the Stone Boat, as well as two private parties. Things happen fast in Expat Land.

Seeking to expand our sound, we added a bassist named Mr. Li and played with a rotating cast of percussionists, including a Mexican, a Canadian, and a Ugandan. One beautiful spring night, Woodie strolled into the Stone Boat accompanied by a tall, lanky guy wearing a traditional Chinese linen jacket.

"This is Zhang Yong," Woodie said. "He is going to play bass with us tonight. I couldn't find Mr. Li."

Zhang Yong looked like a terracotta warrior come to life, with a dignified, classical demeanor and long hair tied into a bun on top of his head. Only the Fender bass slung over his shoulder looked modern. He flashed an easy smile.

We quickly ran through skeleton outlines, and I handed him

a few chord charts I had, but the bassist was basically flying blind and he soared. Zhang Yong's limber, funk-infused style immediately had the rest of us on our toes.

"That was a happy accident," Dave said afterward. "He's great."

Woodie told us that Zhang Yong had just left the pioneering band Zi Yue (Confucius Says) after seven years and they had also met through an instrument repair. We were all pleasantly surprised that he was willing to keep playing with us. His presence made us reach a little higher.

We were still wobbly, though, and only I could tighten things up. I had to overcome my instincts to defer to everyone else because a band needs a leader and everyone was looking to me. I slowly accepted this responsibility, while also beginning to write some original music. I started by playing a simple blues progression and penning a meditation on the city's noxious air. I wanted to express that Beijing was a dirty old town but that it had a grip on me.

> They say the sun is shining, but I don't see it any-
> where . . . I've got the Beijing Blues / I just need a
> gulp of cold clean air.
>    There's stars in my eyes, but I don't see them in
> the sky / This place is under my skin and I wonder
> why oh why.

We settled into a nice routine, playing the Orchard and Stone Boat each once a month. This seemed like the right number of shows to maintain a balance between the band and family life. Becky liked Woodie and knew how much fun I was having. She thought the band was a grand caper after years of hearing me warbling in the living room. She became our gigs' social director, bouncing from table to table, drinking wine and making sure that the wide mix of friends was having fun.

My whole family was getting a kick out of the band and my new role. One night I even lured Jacob up onstage to play hand drums and sing background on "Soulshine," which both of us loved. But I realized that if the music was going to fit with my family lifestyle, I couldn't treat every gig like my twenty-first birthday party, no matter how many people wanted to buy me drinks.

This became obvious when I found myself dragging around the house on a Saturday afternoon following a late-night gig and early soccer wakeup. My head pounded and I longed to crawl into bed, but Eli wanted me to go bike riding with him. When I snapped at him in reply, fear flashed through his eyes and a deep sense of shame washed over me. I decided that moment to quit drinking for a month. Life in Beijing had been one big party, and it was time to give it a rest.

My self-prohibition was interrupted after three weeks by a series of champagne toasts and celebratory parties, fueled by some extraordinary news: Rebecca's bureau had been awarded the Pulitzer Prize for International Reporting for a series called "China's Naked Capitalism."

Winning such an award was fraught with politics, luck, and flukiness, but you have to play to win and Becky had been in the game for a long time, doing great work across a wide spectrum of topics. She had not written the stories but had steered and edited every piece. I viewed the Pulitzer as valida-tion of every grueling hour she had worked, and the care she put into everything she had done since she started her first job in Florida.

Of course, many great journalists do great work for decades and never receive a Pulitzer. Something was in the air. The previous international award had gone to the *New York Times* for its China coverage, and these back-to-back wins confirmed what we had felt since day one: we were in the right place at the right time.

We had been swept up in a giant wave on our first day in Beijing, and the crest just kept rising. We needed to see how far we could ride this thing, and the only way I could see to do that was by keeping our eyes focused directly in front of us.

We had not arrived at this peak as a result of any grand plan but through some holy mixture of luck and pluck. No formula could explain what was happening, and pausing to analyze felt like a recipe for a crash. I messed up a song the second I let my mind wander, and I was certain the same was true for our lives. We had to stay in the moment every moment.

I recalled the wisdom contained in a favorite B.B. King song, which now became my mantra:

*You better not look down if you want to keep on flying.*

# CHAPTER 15

# VISIBLE MAN

'm glad you made it back in one piece."

"Excuse me?"

I had no idea what this guy was talking about, but I was pretty sure I had never seen him before, and certain that we had not traveled anywhere together.

We were standing side by side, playing catch with our sons, warming them up for a baseball game on the fields behind the International School of Beijing. My head was a little foggy from spending the morning coaching two soccer teams, then rushing fifteen minutes north to get Jacob to this baseball game.

He laughed at my confusion. "I'm glad you made it back from your trip to Sichuan. It sounded really scary."

He was referring to my recent column about a perilous bus trip through the sixteen-thousand-foot mountain passes of Sichuan's wild west.

"Oh, thanks." I smiled and threw the ball back to Jacob. "Thanks for reading."

It should have been obvious that he was talking about my column, but I wasn't used to strangers recognizing me or knowing details about my life, even though I shared them widely in my WSJ.com columns and on my personal blog.

I wrote everything desiring readers, but pretending they didn't exist. I had been an open book from the minute I landed in China, but if I pondered my audience too much I would grow self-conscious and hesitant. Though my blog was publicly available, I treated it as an ongoing letter to my family and friends. My openness was puzzling to some, who urged discretion and privacy.

"Stop the madness and think about what you're putting up here," one friend e-mailed. Why, he wondered, was I so willing to post details of my family's ups and down and pictures of my children? I ignored him and anyone else who raised such questions. As a writer I process my thoughts and feelings through chronicling them, and the posts were helping me make sense of everything. Being in China also protected me from becoming overly self-conscious about what I was posting; the website that hosted my blog was usually banned there, so I couldn't read it without a fair amount of effort and neither could anyone else in Beijing. That made it easy to pretend I had no readers.

I wrote about things that interested me without pondering the implications too deeply, and I carried that same spirit over into my WSJ.com columns. Though they were intended for a much wider audience, I still pretended that I was just writing for myself.

This became a progressively harder illusion to maintain as it became clear that Beijing's expats were reading my columns. A friend thinking about transferring her kids to Dulwich visited the school and was handed a copy of a column I had written about my experiences there. This shook me up because I had never intended to pen ad copy. Although happy with the school, we also had plenty of culture-clash annoyances with the administration's British emphasis on athletics, its tone deafness to other sensibilities, and its insistence on uniforms and tucked-in shirts, which I thought represented a more profound emphasis on style over substance.

I could have asked the staff to quit handing out the columns, but I was also flattered and pleased that it would alert newcomers to my work. This typified my deep ambivalence; I wanted everyone to read my column, but I didn't want to be singled out. I wanted my work to be recognized, but I didn't really want to *be* recognized.

My picture ran with the column, however, and strangers began saying hello. One day I was swimming with Eli and Jacob in the Riv's indoor pool when I noticed a guy staring at me. He finally approached and politely asked, "Excuse me, are you Alan Paul?"

"Yes."

"Oh, wow. I'm so honored to meet you."

"Uh, thanks." *Honored? Did he say honored?*

"I love your column. We just moved here and we were so excited when we realized that you lived in Riviera too."

"Oh. Wow. That's really cool. Thank you." *That's weird. Did he say he was excited to live in my compound?*

This meeting was both freaking me out and stroking my ego, but Eli and Jacob just wanted my attention.

"Daddy, throw me!" Eli jumped on my back.

"Yeah," my fan said, as my son climbed up my neck. "We were trying to decide between a few schools and then we read your column about your kids going to Dulwich so we sent them there."

*People were actually choosing their kids' schools based on what I wrote? Maybe I need to weigh my words more carefully.*

Eli leapt off my shoulders. Now he and Jacob both jumped on me, their impatience growing.

"Come on!" Jacob walked his feet up my back.

"Daddy, throwww meeeee!" Eli shouted.

"Well, I better attend to my kids," I said, with one child hanging off each side. "It was really nice to meet you. Thank you for reading and for your support. It means a lot to me."

We shook hands.

"Oh, thank *you*. I was hoping to run into you at school. This is great."

I went back to playing with the kids, tossing them around, but I was distracted. I valued my anonymity—the feeling of nobody knowing me was one of the truly liberating things about moving to Beijing a year earlier. It was strange to feel like people were watching me, but also flattering that anyone cared.

When my boys ran off to get ice cream, I found Becky in the outdoor pool playing with Anna. She laughed at my recounting of the conversation.

"My, my, my," she said. "What have we created?"

Her amusement grew as more people approached me, including once at the airport luggage carousel and another time at a downtown restaurant. Interest grew when the *Journal*'s Chinese-language site began translating the column. On one flight back to New York, a Chinese investment banker across the aisle said he read my column religiously. Most of his colleagues read it as well, he said. They all worked with foreigners but didn't understand us, what we were thinking, or how we were living. I was providing them a valuable window into a strange and mysterious culture, and they enjoyed the chance to view their own country through an American's eyes.

Several times, Rebecca met with Chinese business leaders

who asked if she knew "a man named Paul." With different last names, our connection was not obvious.

I would never hold myself up as a representative of anything, much less my entire country, so I just pushed this out of my mind. What really excited me was how much my experiences resonated with expats and former expats all over, including those living and working in America. I thought I was writing about my China experiences, but I began to appreciate that I was actually documenting what it felt like to live in a different culture.

AT THE TIME we lived in China, there were estimated to be over six million Americans living abroad, and 315,000 in China alone, yet most people in the United States didn't seem to know we existed. I was proud to help normalize this experience, which had been so thoroughly expansive for my entire family, and excited that my readership was growing, but I still had ambivalence about being a public person.

The disadvantage of people noticing me became clear one brutal Monday morning. It began awfully, as we couldn't rouse any of the kids after another weekend when we pushed everything a tad too hard. It felt like a black cloud had settled on the house, with everyone waking up grumpy and unhappy. Jacob was in a particularly foul mood, which didn't lighten as we biked to school together.

Walking into the school lobby, we passed Wyatt Cameron, a teacher and good family friend.

"Hi, Jacob!" he said cheerfully, as my son blew by with a grunt.

"What's wrong with him?" Wyatt asked. "Did he wipe out on the way over here?"

"No," I said. "He's just acting the fool."

Jacob looked at me with fury in his eyes, muttered something about embarrassing him, and stomped away. As I trailed after him, I saw someone walking quickly toward me. It was the guy from the pool.

"Hi, Alan," he said, with an extended hand. There was a smiling woman by his side.

"This is my wife. She also loves your column."

I shook hands and said hello to both. As much as I appreciated their support, I needed to focus on Jacob, who was still a couple of steps ahead of me. "It's really nice to meet you," I said, "but I'm sorry, I just can't talk right now. My son is having a rough morning."

"Yeah," Jacob barked, turning his head over his shoulder. "Because of you!"

We walked into the bathroom together and I told him to take a deep breath.

"I don't know what's bugging you," I said. "But you need to calm down and get to class."

Jacob has always had an amazing knack for pulling himself together for school, no matter what was going on and he did it again, apologizing sheepishly and giving me a little hug before heading to class. I turned to the sink to splash water on my face. At 8:00 a.m., it had already been a long day. I looked into the mirror and didn't like what I saw.

With no time to put my contact lenses on, I was wearing my chunky black-framed glasses, along with old yoga pants and a threadbare Pittsburgh Pirates T-shirt. My hair was sticking up at odd angles and I badly needed a shave. I was stressed out and badly undercaffeinated, and it showed all over my face. I wondered if seeing me like this, and in conflict with my son, would alter my readers' impressions. Then I was shocked to even ponder such a thing.

Did it matter if readers saw my underbelly? Did I have to start contemplating my appearance every time I left the house, or try to put a happy face on anything I was going through? I would never do that. The column's success stemmed from being willing to be honest and cut close to the bone. I wasn't going to change a thing.

# CHAPTER 16

# INTO THE MYSTIC

Language misunderstandings were part of my life in China from the day I arrived until the day I left. The more I attempted to get out and really speak Chinese, the more I opened myself to screwing things up. Usually, these mishaps just led to annoyances or minor mistakes, like taking a roundabout cab ride or ordering the wrong dishes in a restaurant.

Sometimes, however, the foul-ups were downright hilarious, as when I tried to purchase edamame at a local market. It began with a comment by Theo Yardley, who walked in for a visit one day when I was cooking frozen edamame for my kids. She saw what I was doing and advised me that fresh soybeans were readily available at local markets. They were called *mao dou*, or hairy beans, she said, referring to the soft fuzz that covers them.

A few days later I was buying fruits and vegetables in the large warehouse behind the Kite Market when I remembered this conversation. Unable to remember the name, I called Theo. When she did not answer her phone, I stretched my brain as far as I could and remembered that *mao* meant hair, but I could not recall how to say bean. Suddenly, the word popped into my head—*bi* (pronounced "be").

I approached the young woman at the stand where I had just purchased cilantro, carrots, and celery, smiled, and said, "*Ni hao. Ni yo mao bi ma?*" ("Hello. Do you have any edamame?" Or so I thought.) She grinned oddly and shook her head no, so I moved along, going to a series of stands and asking the same thing, always with the same result.

After five or six such requests, I was about to give up when Theo returned my call.

"Hey, what's up?" she asked.

"Oh, nothing. I was wondering how you say edamame, but I remembered it was *mao bi*," I said proudly.

There was a silence followed by a short, sharp guffaw. "Did you ask for that?"

"Yes," I said. "But no one seems to have it."

My friend burst out laughing and it took her thirty seconds to regain her composure enough to speak. "Oh, Alan," she said. "I think you should head home now. You made a big mistake. It's, uh . . ."

Theo was having a hard time spitting out the nature of my blunder. My mind raced trying to figure out what I had said, and I felt the blood drain from my face as I remembered where I had heard the word *bi*—it was a central part of an X-rated cheer that Chinese crowds liked to chant in national team competitions against Japan. It was a vulgar term for the female genitalia. I had been asking a series of young women if they had any hairy vaginas.


OBVIOUSLY, I HAD a lot to learn, and I probably should have increased my Chinese course load, but I could not bring myself to do so. After Tom left, I found the classes to be melancholy reminders of the circumstances surrounding his absence. Even as I tried to get over that, I simply got busier and found myself studying less and less, even though I was falling ever more in love with China and wanted to speak to everyone about everything.

I soon dropped learning characters to focus on the oral language. You simply cannot master written Chinese without hours of serious studying, and I was not properly committed to doing so; there were too many other things I wanted to do.

My teacher Yechen was disappointed, and he told me that his professor in London had given him one staunch piece of advice about teaching Chinese privately: do not take any students who refuse to learn characters because it indicated a lack of seriousness. Still, we continued, and my language skills progressed steadily. As much as anything, I just liked spending time with Yechen, gaining insight into his view of China's history and its contemporary potential and problems.

He believed that modern China was lost, raising a generation of people cut off from their long, proud history. Chinese society was based on the principles espoused in Confucianism, Taoism, and Buddhism, he said, and too few people now understood what that meant and were caught up in an endless quest for material things.

Yechen was thoroughly grounded in classical Chinese philosophy, culture, and religion. He spoke in aphorisms without pretension, animated his conversation with references to ancient parables, guided his decision making by looking to historical precedence, and was obviously out of step with contemporary Beijing's go-go aesthetic. But he was also full of contradictory impulses, an Anglophile from his time in London who had cultured taste in music and literature, both Western (Tennessee Williams) and Chinese (the intellectual

Gao Xingjian)—and displayed a simple but distinct sarto-rial flair. As someone who has always enjoyed big, eccentric personalities, I found all this entirely endearing.

Yechen only had a couple of other students, preferring to focus on reading and writing. He had dozens of composition books filled with his journals, rows and rows of meticulous calligraphy characters. Though I could not read them, I believed that they were likely filled with brilliant insights, and I hoped that he managed to achieve his dream of turning them into a book.

Chinese people seemed to have a harder time relating to Yechen. When he came to my house, Yechen often spoke with our two *ayi*s, sometimes at length. They respected him as a *laoshi*, or teacher, and seemed to enjoy chatting with him, but they both thought he was strange. He was clearly very bright, Hou Ayi told me, so why didn't he have a better job or higher ambitions?

During my second year studying with Yechen, we started visiting some of his favorite places around Beijing together. One day we visited a small Buddhist temple and the White Cloud Temple (*Baiyunguan*), Beijing's most revered Taoist site, where a monk friend of his lived and studied. Yechen had already given me a couple of books about Buddhism, which he practiced. But he was lately talking more about Taoism as well, and he was beginning to explain the relationship between these two religions to me.

According to Yechen, Buddhism had been a flexible religion, adopting the characters of the dominant religions everywhere it spread from India. So Tibetan Buddhism was mystical, based on the Bon religion that predated it, and Chinese Buddhism was grounded in Taoism, which was firmly established when Buddhism arrived.

"Taoism is the root and Buddhism is the flower," he explained. "They are part of the same system."

He met me at a subway stop and we strolled over to the White Cloud Temple, a large, beautiful complex with a quiet, peaceful feel. He told me that it was spared throughout the Cultural Revolution because many of the communist government's top leaders secretly prayed here, arriving in the middle of the night. This has gone on for decades, he said, and continues today. The Chinese Taoist Association was headquartered here, which protected the site, but also left it vulnerable to government control and corruption. Because the concept of feng shui stems from Taoism, and remains very important to many secular Chinese, who will pay monks high fees to help them properly design their homes, money flows through Taoist temples.

Monk dorm rooms lined the side of the temple in between shrines. Yechen knocked gently on the door of one room, where his friend answered and ushered us into a tiny space. It was just big enough for two beds and two small desks, with a tiny bit of floor space in between.

The friend, Wang, was wearing the normal Taoist monk outfit, with his long hair tied in a bun atop his head underneath a small brown cap, almost like an old-fashioned nurse's hat, and a brown robe wrapped around him. He turned on a water kettle and carefully, gently filled a small teapot with leaves. As we waited for the water to boil, I looked around and noticed the beautiful Chinese calligraphy hanging above the desk. Yechen explained that his friend had done all of them. He urged me to speak Chinese, and I did my best to engage in conversation with the quiet Wang.

The tea was delicious, rich and multilayered, and we drank countless tiny cups before rising, saying our thanks, and heading out for a detailed tour of the grounds. Yechen whispered conspiratorially about government plots making a lot of money off the temple—"fake monks" who profiteered on the backs of the true believers. I feared that he might be a little nuts and conspiracy minded until, on the way out, we saw a Taoist monk exit the temple and climb into the driver's seat of a black Audi. I looked over at Yechen, and he raised his eyebrows. "See?" he whispered. "Many, many fake monks here."

After a vegetarian lunch at a nearby restaurant—"we can't go into these temples with meat on our breath," he said—we turned down a winding road that led into a hutong. These narrow, old alleyway streets used to cover central Beijing but were now being torn down at a remarkable and depressing pace. Most of them were too narrow to accept more than a trickle of motorized traffic, making them islands of calm; they were almost always replaced with towering glass skyscrapers and traffic-clogged, multilane roads.

We passed by many little bakeries making *baozi*, the big soft dough balls that are a popular Beijing street food. We were followed by a pack of omnipresent hutong dogs, the amazing little mutts who roam all over Beijing's old neighborhoods. I looked up on the roof and saw a series of cats also running along with us. Toddlers bundled up for winter peered out from behind their parents' large baozi delivery bikes. I felt a million miles away from everything, but closely observed.

We passed a large recycling station, which you see all over Beijing, tucked into the city's poorer, more remote corners. People ride large flat-backed three-wheeled bikes all around to pick up recyclable material—cardboard, glass, tin, aluminum, and plastic, often including giant cooking oil bottles tied together and rattling around. Their bikes often look ready to topple over. Migrant workers at these little centers buy and sort the goods, which they then sell themselves. It looked like the family running this center slept there, under a plastic tarp set up as a makeshift home.

Chinese New Year was just days away and the city was buzzing. Little stands selling boxes of fruit to give as presents were everywhere, along with fireworks stands. On New Year's Eve, there would be an orgy of explosions.

Chinese New Year is the most important holiday. It is like Thanksgiving, Christmas, New Year's, and the Fourth of July wrapped up into one. Everyone who possibly can returns to his or her hometown, causing the largest annual migration of people in the world, with hundreds of millions of people criss-crossing China. Throughout the city, the energy of so many people moving with purpose was palpable, but in this hutong, life was ticking at its normal pace.

"Look around," Yechen said. "These are the people too poor to travel home."

He himself would not be returning to his hometown of Wuxi, near Shanghai, though he often spoke of his mother.

At the entrance to the Buddhist temple, a little old man sat inside a ticket booth. I looked over his shoulder and laughed, seeing that the walls were plastered with *Slam* posters of dunking NBA stars like Kevin Garnett, Kobe Bryant, and LeBron James

"Do you like basketball?" I asked in Chinese.

"Oh yes, very much," he said.

"I work for that magazine," I said, pointing. He smiled and waved me in, which surprised me and impressed Yechen. This was the second time *Slam* had greased the wheels for me in Beijing.

Yechen showed me around the temple, taking me into shrines and teaching me the proper way to light incense and place it in the giant burners, and how to pray before a golden Buddha. This graven idol worship stirred no guilt in my Jewish soul. I just tried to follow Yechen and imagine what he was feeling inside.

THREE WEEKS LATER, Yechen asked me if I wanted to accompany him and his monk friend Wang on a pilgrimage to Huashan, one of Taoism's five holy mountains, located near Xi'an in central China. Many people consider it the heart and soul of the Taoist religion. It sounded like an unforgettable journey, but my family already had plans, so Yechen went with another of his students, returning deeply moved.

He told me all about the harrowing hike up to Huashan's five peaks and showed me photos of single-plank walkways along sheer cliffs suspended by chains above steep drops. The peaks were shrouded in mist and dotted with small stone temples and stunted evergreens. His enthusiasm made perfect sense.

About a month later, Yechen sat down for a lesson and told me he would be leaving Beijing. He had a great job offer from another London university, with a high salary and free lodging in a storied Victorian mansion. He often spoke longingly about his time in London, so I thought this was great news, but when I congratulated him, he said he wasn't sure he would accept the position. He had been profoundly moved by that trip to Huashan and was giving serious thought to becoming a monk instead.

As we discussed this further, it became clear to me that he was restrained only by guilt about his mother's reaction. "Chinese parents don't want their kids to be monks," he explained. Chinese born in the last thirty years, since the nation instituted its one-child policy, felt tremendous pressure not to disappoint their parents. The monk's vow of celibacy meant no grand-children and the unofficial vow of poverty meant no long-term financial support for the parents, who lack an American-style social security system.

When he asked my opinion, I told him rather tepidly that he should go to London. I thought being a monk sounded like a wild gambit, but I hesitated to really share my feelings because I didn't want to insult him.

I thought about Yechen constantly over the five days before our next class. The more I did, the crazier becoming a monk seemed and the more inadequate I considered my milquetoast response. He was obviously unhappy and looking for a change. But renouncing the material world was too radical. Going to London might well turn things around, and if not, he could always return to China and enter the monkhood. If he chose that route first, however, it would be much harder to change course. I developed a coherent argument and was prepared to have a good talk.

WHEN YECHEN RETURNED to my house, he promptly an-nounced that he had rejected the London offer and would soon be searching for a monastery. I wanted to try to talk him out of this until he told me that over the weekend he had visited the White Cloud Temple and ceremoniously burned all those me-ticulous diaries. A chill ran through me as he said that he had come to see the journals as totems of youthful naïveté, markers of a past he was leaving behind.

"I thought I would feel sadness and fear when I burned them," he said. "But I felt a great sense of release and peace."

I hoped that the feeling would continue, but I was concerned. He said that he would travel with one small bag, going from place to place until he found a place that suited him. All of his friends thought him crazy, he said. I did not consider Yechen insane, but his vision of monkhood seemed awfully romantic, like a mythical American kid talking about setting out with his baseball glove and bat until he found some nirvana where he could play ball round the clock. I was shaken that he hadn't decided whether to be a Buddhist or Taoist monk, which seemed to cry out that he was seeking escape more than true spiritual enlightenment.

A few days later, we met for lunch at a vegetarian restaurant near the Lama Temple, Beijing's largest Tibetan Buddhist site.

"Chinese people today think that only someone who is a failure would become a monk," Yechen said, echoing what I had been hearing from Chinese friends. "They think it is opting out of life. But I don't feel that way.

"Everyone is concerned about being cheated by someone else, but it doesn't matter."

This was a radical statement, which got to the heart of something I saw all the time in China; everyone lived in constant fear that they were being ripped off. This anxiety was most obvious in market shopping, where people bargained like their lives depended on it, but it also seeped through much of life. I found myself constantly fighting that way of thinking; it was one aspect of going native that I wanted no part of.

"They should worry about cheating themselves instead, which is the worst crime you can commit," he said. "If I didn't do this, I would be cheating myself."

He spoke so convincingly and in such a clearheaded manner that I started to feel guilty about my own doubts.

When I said I was happy for him, but would miss him greatly, he smiled faintly then brushed away my sentiment.

"There are many good teachers," he said. "You won't have a problem finding one."

We both took bites of vegetable dumplings before I countered with a simple truth: "Sure. But it won't be the same."

"Yes," he admitted.

Aware it was the last time we would see each other for a long time, we were speaking more openly than usual. "The problem with most Chinese teachers—with most young Chinese—is they lack an understanding of the deep and real culture here. Let's be honest, you're going to forget the language when you go back to America anyhow."

After two years, he was acknowledging the eight-hundred-pound gorilla in the room; I would forget everything I was studying. This cynical thought had pushed me to skip over any word or grammar rule for which I didn't see an immediate use, but I had never dared express it to Yechen.

"But the language is a bridge to the culture," he continued. "And the culture can stay with you forever."

# CHAPTER 17

# BRINGING IT ALL BACK HOME

On our second summer break in the United States we drove more than two thousand miles in a rented minivan. I slept in a dozen beds, including a Spider-Man trundle next to my cousin's six-year-old son and a pop-up camper in my in-laws' backyard. It was exhausting, but at every stop we reconnected with parents, brothers, sisters, aunts, uncles, nephews, and nieces—cementing the relationships we swore we would not forsake when we moved to China.

In Pittsburgh I played a gig with my father's Dixieland band. He was taking great delight in my burgeoning music career in Beijing, claiming full credit and laughing at how close my apple had fallen to his tree. Sitting next to him faking my way through jazz standards like "All of Me" and "Satin Doll," I recalled the fear and dread that infused saying good-bye to my dad on my first visit home from China. Sitting and playing music with him sixteen months later was a simple, sublime pleasure.

One of the most important reconnections we made on that whole journey came in Washington, D.C., during the only three days we spent without any extended family. We were getting back in touch with what it means to be American. After two years studying in the British curriculum, nine-year-old Jacob knew a lot about ancient Rome, Greece, Britain, and China, but his knowledge of American history was lacking. He had stared blankly when we asked him about George Washington and Abraham Lincoln a few months earlier. We largely remedied this shortcoming with a collection of books, but he and seven-year-old Eli needed a deeper understanding.

A surge of patriotic emotion hit me as soon as we stepped out of a cab in front of the floodlit Washington Monument and looked over at the Capitol. My feelings caught me off guard; I had spent so much time thinking about how the trip would impact the kids that I forgot how living abroad might heighten my own sensitivities and appreciation.

Being an expat can complicate your feelings about being American. We tend to possess an assumed superiority that I only noticed when it was punctured. I was also jarred by the commercialism that could engulf anything in the United States. Everything from a McDonald's Happy Meal to a spider exhibit at New York's Museum of Natural History was a marketing opportunity for the latest Hollywood blockbuster. I was overwhelmed by the simple act of walking into a grocery store, blinking under the bright fluorescent lights, and staring at the massive, overstocked aisles.

Living in a place like China also gives you a much greater appreciation for simple liberties you take for granted growing up in America. I wasn't quite sure what the children felt in Washington, but they understood where we were.

Before we entered the Vietnam Veterans Memorial, I explained to the kids what it was and said it was like visiting a graveyard and that they should treat it with the same level of respect. I pondered explaining how Vietnam was close to China and that America had been there fighting the spread of a government very similar to that under which our family had now chosen to live, but that just seemed like too much information.

Seven-year-old Eli walked slowly with a hushed reverence even as the other kids rushed through. Amazed to find our own first names engraved on the wall—"There's a Jacob! There's an Alan!"—he asked why people had left flowers and flags and if we had any relatives who died in the war. Then he asked, "Even though we didn't really know anyone, could we leave a flower for them, too?"

I told him it was a beautiful idea. He ran out of the memorial, plucked some clovers from the lawn, and returned.

"What do I do, Dad?"

"Put them down on the ground and say a prayer for one of the soldiers, or even for all of them on that section."

"How do I say a prayer for them?"

"You say something like, 'God, please grant peace to these soldiers, who gave their lives for our country, and to their families, who still miss them very much.'"

He meticulously placed a flower into the crack of the wall and shut his eyes for a few seconds.

When he was done, I gave him a big hug and we walked out together.

But even in D.C., with my own nationalism running high, I had moments that made me question where home really was. At the National Zoo panda exhibit, there was a slide show of the bears' Sichuan home, which we had visited just months earlier. Looking at the pictures of smiling Chinese peasants, mist-shrouded hills, and dilapidated general stores, I felt homesickness for China.

. . . .

WE HAD A gig scheduled a week after my return to Beijing —at the Orchard on my forty-first birthday. Woodie had not responded to my repeated e-mails asking him to line up a new drummer. Lacking a mobile e-mail device, I jumped online to check my messages as soon as we arrived at a new destination. I read Woodie's response with my laptop perched on my knee on the back porch of a rented house at the Jersey Shore, the one spot where I could receive pirated wi-fi.

> Found a drummer who should be good. Want to get to-
> gether to discuss the band when you return.

That sounded ominous. He and Zhang Yong had begun playing in a hard rock band with a charismatic singer, and I assumed that had taken flight while I was away. I was sure he was ready to move on, but replied simply:

> Great on the drummer. Look forward to talking.

With a strong sense that we might not have much life left as a band, I tried to look at the bright side: we had gotten further than I thought possible. If it ended there, so be it.

# CHAPTER 18

# BIT BY BIT (LITTLE BY LITTLE)

I used to think that jet lag was a crock. I had always believed in getting on a plane, setting my watch to the time in the destination city, and not looking back. I refused to even consider what time it was somewhere I wasn't and truly believed that anyone's internal clock could be reset with a combination of sheer will and proper beverage management—a strategic, properly timed intake of coffee, beer, and water.

But that was before I found myself trying to put together a massive Playmobil castle at 3:00 a.m. with kids crawling all over me. I still believed that any adult could power through anything, but it was impossible to watch how jet lag flipped my children on their heads and argue against it being a serious blow to the body.

Our first night back in Beijing, Jacob woke up at midnight, climbed into our bed, and flopped around for half an hour before I dragged myself up and launched a computer game for him. I drifted back to sleep before hearing Anna talking to her older brother. When I got back up, I found Jacob alone and asked where Anna was.

"Upstairs," he said, not taking his eyes off the computer screen, where he was slaying aliens. "Eli's taking care of her."

I nodded, mumbled, and got back in bed. Then I realized that my seven-year-old was in charge of my four-year-old and trudged up to the third floor to have a look.

"Hi, Dad," Eli exclaimed. "Now that you're up, you can put my castle together!"

I started reading the instructions of this thing, which we had dragged all the way back from Pittsburgh, before realizing that it wasn't yet 4:00 a.m. and I badly needed some coffee. I thought of the six pounds of Peet's I brought back, and headed downstairs to brew a pot, wordlessly acknowledging that my night's sleep was over.

It took over a week to fully conquer this beast, so I was still foggy headed when I rode downtown for an afternoon rehearsal, where I would meet our new drummer and have that dreaded meeting with Woodie.

We met in a basement studio in the subterranean depths underneath a KFC. The place was accessed by walking through a dingy garage and down a stinky hallway that led to a filthy bathroom. The studio was run by the members of a band who were in it for free rehearsal space.

I walked into the clean little room and a stocky, barrel-chested guy with a big smile jumped up from behind the drum kit to say hello. Woodie introduced me to Lu Wei, who had a neatly trimmed beard but no mustache and was wearing a baseball hat pulled down low over hip rectangular glasses.

Zhang Yong waved and smiled without standing up from his stool, his trusty Fender bass perched on his lap. Woodie gave me a tiny handshake. Hellos and good-byes with Chinese friends were often awkward because they tended to come and go without much fanfare. Handshakes were rare and hugs

were definitely out. But the awkwardness only lasted two minutes—until we started playing.

A drummer exerts tremendous control over a band's flow,
and Lu Wei was on a different plane than anyone else we had
played with. It was like having Magic Johnson stroll onto your
basketball team and take over point guard duties; everyone
else started running a little harder. After a spirited two-hour
rehearsal, Woodie and I said bye to Lu Wei and Zhang Yong
and walked upstairs to the sparkling clean KFC. We got Cokes
and sat down amid a sea of uniformed schoolkids stopping in
for an afternoon snack on their way home.

I was torn between enthusiasm about what we had just done
and anxiety about what he would say.

"So what do you want to talk about?" I sipped from my drink.

"I was watching some videos of our gigs while you were
gone," Woodie said.

*Uh-oh.*

"And I think we can be really good—if you're willing to
practice regularly and work on original music. What do you
think?"

I thought I was going to fall off my chair, but I played it
cool. "I think I'd like that very much."


WE HAD TWO gigs the following Saturday. In the afternoon,
we played on a large stage inside a hotel courtyard in the hip,
fast-gentrifying Nan Luo Gu Xiang hutong as part of Beijing's
first modern street festival. We were asked to submit, for government approval, copies of all the lyrics we would be singing,
but Woodie told me not to worry about what I handed over,
confident it would all just be shoved into a file and forgotten.
"Give them a lot of stuff about love," he advised.

Our opening acts were a trio of elderly traditional Chinese musicians and an ancient man who told jokes and sang folk songs, accompanying himself on a one-stringed instrument. Much to my kids' delight, he only had one tooth.

One of the promoters, a wiry Frenchman, approached as we were about to go onstage. "Look at that," he said, turning to point to the large local crowd milling around the courtyard entrance. "Can you try to draw them closer?"

I asked Woodie to handle that in Chinese, but he declined. "You ask them first, in English. They'll like that," he said. "If they're still back there after one song, I'll ask."

As we played our opening chords, I motioned with my arm, and said, "Ni hao. Please come closer. We want to see you." Everyone pushed forward and rushed to the lip of the stage, where my kids were sitting. I tried to channel the adrenaline that surged through me into the music.

This was the first time we had played for a mostly Chinese audience, the first time we had played in daylight, and one of the few times my kids had been there. I was happy for them to see me onstage and to take in this whole scene. A handful of Chinese teenagers stood right in front looking at me in awe, like I was a rock star. I shut my eyes behind dark sunglasses and tried to really let go.

Afterward, Dave left with his family, saying he would see us in a few hours. Becky and I took the kids down the hutong for a soda, a slice of fresh watermelon, and a bag of freshly popped popcorn—sweet instead of salty, the norm in China. They seemed to enjoy watching us play, and I loved having them there, but they weren't particularly wowed by the experience.

I walked them out to our car, kissed everyone good-bye, and headed back to meet up with Woodie, Lu Wei, and Zhang Yong in a cool little hutong bar, where they were settled into overstuffed couches, beer mugs in their hands. It was our first time hanging out without instruments in our hands. With Yechen gone, I thought, maybe these guys were going to be my new guides to China. It would be a very different tour.

Three Chinese hippies began playing music on the street: a bear of a man with a dreadlocked beard tied into a point and hanging down to his belly button strummed a ukulele; a short dreadlocked guy pounded a conga drum; and a wispy little fellow alternated between a uke and a small plastic keyboard with a mouthpiece attached. He was wearing the brightly colored clothes common in the villages we had visited in Guizhou and nodded yes when I asked if he was Miao. Woodie played harmonica for a few songs, then I grabbed my guitar. A large crowd gathered as I played along, then led the band through three songs.

When I walked back inside, Lu Wei and Zhang Yong said something I didn't understand, then broke up laughing.

"They said that you made those guys sound like Alan music," Woodie translated. "It sounded better than they thought it would."

Our little group kept expanding, as cousins, girlfriends and friends arrived. With Dave gone, I was the lone Westerner, and it struck me that this feeling of being a distinct minority is what living in China should feel like every day.

I wanted to take everyone out to dinner to thank them for playing for free that afternoon, but I only had 160 RMB (about $22) and we were nowhere near an ATM. Our party of nine walked down the hutong and entered a little restaurant that was pure old Beijing. Woodie took the menu and ordered spicy tofu, gong bao chicken, fried noodles, sautéed potatoes, and some other comfort foods, as well as a round of giant bottles of Tsingtao. The food was simple and delicious.

When the bill was dropped on the table, I picked it up and

did a double take. The total was 79 RMB, about $11—just over $1 per person. I was able to take everyone out after all. The same night, Becky had dinner with friends at one of the city's hippest new restaurants, a massive glass structure designed by a French artist, where they paid $40 per entrée for limp, uninspired Western cuisine. The extreme contrast between our meals summed up a lot about life in Beijing, where many different economies and worlds existed side by side.

At the Stone Boat, Woodie told me that his friend Powell Young, the "Chinese king of shred guitar," was there. "Shred" is a form of extremely fast, pyrotechnic guitar playing that peaked in the late 1980s and early 1990s. The demanding style retained a dedicated core of devotees, and I had spent plenty of time writing about it for *Guitar World*. The idea of having the king of Chinese shred join us seemed both hilarious and awesome. I told Woodie to pick a song and call him up.

"He plays really wild and fast."

"Can't he control himself and fit in?"

"I don't think so. When he's onstage, he's in the spotlight. That's the only way he knows."

"Just go for it when the moment seems right."

We were loose and comfortable from an afternoon of hanging out together and confident because we had just played. By the time we took the stage for our second set, at about 11:30, the large crowd on the outer patio had cleared and only about twenty-five people remained, most of them Woodie's friends.

As we launched into the tribal rhythm of our final song, "Not Fade Away," a Buddy Holly tune fueled by a furious Bo Diddley beat, Woodie locked eyes with Powell and gestured for him. As Dave played a honking solo, Powell, who was sitting inside drinking with a gang of friends, ran up and took the guitar out of Woodie's hands.

Powell began playing a solo that grew increasingly fevered and outlandish. His right, picking hand flew up the neck to join his left hand, and he let fly a barrage of tapped notes, a difficult technique that allows you to play with eye-popping speed. Lu Wei started going wild, playing extravagant drum fills while pushing the rhythm and driving Powell deeper into frenzy.

I was banging the simple two-chord rhythm, with Zhang Yong behind me, laughing and laying down a deep, funky bass line. Our thunderous racket boomed through the otherwise empty park. Everyone inside the small club, including the bartenders and owner Jonathan Ansfield, ran out to stand on the porch and cheer us on. Woodie stood in the middle, a beer in his hand, laughing.

Two sets of middle-aged German parents and their teen sons occupied the table directly in front of us, one man sucking thoughtfully on a pipe all night, like a caricature of a European professor. Now they had a front-row seat to this madness. The teens jumped up and started screaming, followed by their parents, who joined in a crazy, spastic dance.

Powell walked off the stage, sat down opposite the pipe smoker, smiled at him, and kept playing. When he finally strolled back to the stage and we brought the song down to a crashing ending, after a twenty-minute guitar solo, the small crowd erupted in a huge ovation.

We hopped off the stage and I shook hands with the Germans, who thanked us and headed home. It was almost 1:00 a.m. but the band stuck around drinking beer for an hour in the otherwise empty, serene park. We were riding a high from the electric finale to a momentous twelve hours in the life of our little band. Though we didn't discuss it, we all understood that things were changing: I was now fronting a Chinese band;

we were becoming more than a bunch of guys who met up to play music together; and we suddenly sounded like we had the potential to really grow into something.

It was almost 2:00 a.m. when Dave and I walked out of the park, dragging our gear behind us. We banged on the window of the little shack by the gate to wake up a young guard sleeping on a cot. He jumped up to let us out and we climbed into Dave's Volvo wagon. His driver, waiting by its side, was a sweet sight at the end of a long day.

"We're making some moves," I told Dave, as we watched the city fly by. The streets of Beijing were filled with cement trucks at this hour, rumbling to and from giant construction sites, which were lit up by banks of floodlights and humming all night.

"Yes, we are. Now your job is to keep Lu Wei happy."

I stumbled inside my house, dumped my guitar and gear bag by the front door, and collapsed into bed. Six hours later, I was on the soccer field coaching first Eli, then Jacob. I didn't have much voice left and was sucking down coffee to keep me alert. Sweating profusely, I ran up and down the soccer pitch yelling instructions at kids. Last night's pseudo rock star had been transformed into a schlepping international dad with deep, dark bags under his eyes.

# CHAPTER 19

# THEM CHANGES

**M**y day-to-day existence was being transformed, with the band moving from a fun little side project into a far more central place in my life. This all felt normal in Beijing, where growth and change were the only constants and anything felt possible.

I had even taken up hockey, despite not having skated in twenty years. A dozen of us who had never held a stick before took up the sport after Canadian friends turned some nearby tennis courts into a mini ice rink. We improved rapidly and soon actually considered ourselves hockey players, resenting our group's official name: "Monday Night Learn to Skate."

None of this reinvention felt disorienting. Not in Beijing, where the whole landscape was being transformed. I would have had to spin a cocoon and emerge as a butterfly to match my surroundings' pace of change. In this atmosphere, sitting still or staying the same would have been the strangest, most radical move of all.

In that environment, remaking yourself—just hitting the reset button and starting over—seemed like the most natural thing in the world. It was happening all around me: there was the journalist running restaurants and bars; the doctor with a thriving export business; the teacher designing T-shirts; the Italian musician selling antique furniture; the Boston bakery owner hanging his shingle as a sports marketer; and the British banker directing an art museum. Anything felt possible, and the only crime was setting your sights too low.

The whole sprawling metro area often felt like a giant construction site, literally evolving in front of our eyes, making life in our Rust Belt hometowns seem positively glacial. Even in New York, projects like the World Trade Center site could take years to get off the ground.

When we arrived in Beijing two years earlier, our compound sat on the edge of urban sprawl, with the countryside lapping up against the walls. Now, many humble local businesses had been replaced by higher-end establishments; fields had become shops, compounds, and highways; and the formerly dusty, dingy Jing Shun Lu was lined with trees, bushes, and flowers after a beautification spurred by the Olympics. I saw sections of the road transformed from morning to evening.

When a friend mentioned that a major construction project had begun on a quiet country road lined with fields and man-made fishing holes, I jumped on my bike and pedaled over. The field was filled with earthmovers, cranes, huge drilling machines, and dozens of workers. The farmers who usually dried their corn there in the fall were nowhere to be seen. Pylons were rising for an elevated highway that would transform the area, with flyways and a massive concrete structure cutting through what was now a village, many small businesses, light industry, and farmland. Dust already covered everything, and blocks of businesses, homes, and factories had been reduced to piles of bricks, which were being carted away by mule-drawn carriages.

I wondered about the displaced people and mourned the loss of the country vibe—I liked the feeling of living on the frontier. But I refused to talk about how things used to be; I'd only been there two years myself. Everyone's view of "normal" starts the moment they arrive, and the one thing that wasn't going to change in Beijing was the constant change.

Wanting to document all this in a column, I spent a day driving around with a translator, asking people what they thought about the new highway. Inside the Kite Market, some vendors said the highway would bring more customers, but most insisted that it wouldn't affect them—though the construction was literally casting a shadow on them. They all spoke with an odd mix of fatalism and optimism I couldn't relate to. They believed that they couldn't do much about whatever was happening and it would probably be for the best anyhow.

I returned days later with Hou Ayi to buy produce and was rocked by how things had changed in the week since I visited to record the rapid pace of change. Half of the parking lots and all the vendors who had worked in them were gone. I looked at the paving bricks being carted away on mule carts and wondered what had happened to the vendors I was so used to seeing.

Where was the lady who sold me the little turtle for Anna? The butcher selling pigs' hearts? The peasant fruit vendors who had asked how much of a fine I had to pay for having three kids in America, and couldn't understand why I didn't have at least five if the government didn't stop me? None of them were anywhere to be seen, and the remaining vendors claimed to have no idea where they had gone.

. . . .

WE WERE PLAYING as many gigs as we could. I had long since forgotten my pledge to only perform twice a month. That now felt like a rationalization for not being able to get more shows. I started bugging Woodie to find us a local spot to play, and on a cool Friday night, we debuted at Jianghu Jiuba, a small courtyard bar nestled deep in a downtown hutong that was virtually impossible to find.

You entered Jianghu through a small stone entryway, covered in the colder months with a heavy blanket, and walked down a short hallway into a charming courtyard, filled with a few picnic tables. A bar nestled against the back wall. To the left was a small room with a foosball game and a few tables usually occupied by young, hip Chinese who were playing cards, strumming acoustic guitars, sipping tea or beer, and smoking like chimneys. To the right of the courtyard, through a French door, was a rectangular room that could squeeze in fifty people. A tiny stage sat in front. There were no toilets; to relieve yourself, you had to walk about twenty yards down the dark hutong to public facilities. The owner was Woodie's former bandmate, a happy-go-lucky hippie saxophonist from Guizhou named Tianxiao.

I was in love with the place the first time I walked in. Because it was run largely by and for musicians, the small room had a great sound system that carried the music throughout the whole place. On the way home, Dave and I were in agreement: it had been a magical night. When I met Woodie, I had hoped he would introduce me to the music scene, but I never could have guessed that he would pull me into its very core.

In the morning, I told Becky about the place and how half the crowd was musicians who got up to jam. A cup of black coffee sat in front of me on our kitchen table next to Becky's glass of water and a half-eaten banana.

"I would have been happy just to have found that place," I said. "Being the band that all those guys were listening to and jamming with was almost too much. I had to struggle to just focus on playing."

Becky laughed. Just back from a run, she was coated in sweat and stretching her calves. We could hear the boys watching *Star Wars* in the family room across the hall and Anna pushing a toy shopping cart through the hallway with a friend who had slept over.

"That's great," she said. "It sounds like a really cool place. I'll come next time you play there."

"That would be great."

I took a sip of coffee and stumbled on my next sentence. "Um, tonight . . . I . . . tonight . . ."

"Are you playing there again tonight? We are going to a family dinner to welcome some new journalists to town."

"No, I'm not playing there, but I did agree to, um . . . two different gigs. I'm sorry. I can still go to the dinner and leave from there."

I was ready to take my lumps. I had crossed a line by booking three gigs in two days, violating the unspoken protocol that weekends were sacred family time, and I had done it without any discussion. That's why I had such a hard time spitting it out.

My parents knew all about the dangers of spousal abandonment that playing in a band posed, and they had both warned me to be careful, but I was too caught up to pay much heed. When a new restaurant offered Woodie $300 for a duo acoustic performance, I was seduced by the fact that anyone wanted to hire us for this kind of show and agreed, even though I didn't really want to do it. Later in the night, I had committed to performing again with the jazz band for Danny Pearl World Music Night, the same event that had lit my musical fuse a year earlier.

Becky took a drink of her water, put the glass down in the sink, and turned back to face me. She did not hide her annoyance, but she was gentle. For years I had held down the familial fort no matter where her job took her, how late she came home, or how early she left. We both understood I was making some withdrawals now.

"I know how fun this is and how much it means to you, and you guys really sound a lot better than I thought possible," she said. "But please remember that you can say no."

# CHAPTER 20

# I WILL DARE

**S**aying no proved to be difficult. Tianxiao asked us to play every Friday night as the Jianghu Jiuba house band, and I wanted to do it because the place fascinated and energized me. Playing in front of a Chinese crowd liberated my singing, as the self-consciousness of being a white man singing the blues receded. I felt like a true folk musician sharing my American heritage—like I had a legit claim to the music. Dave also loved playing here, and the crowd was deeply appreciative of his soulful playing.

Dave was a couple of years older than I, with an impressive head of salt-and-pepper hair. We both laughed when Woodie told us after one show at Jianghu that one of his friends said, "The old guy has a lot of soul."

Unfortunately, we had to turn Tianxiao down because the club only paid us cab fare of about 100 RMB ($14) per person, and Zhang Yong had a regular money gig playing cover songs at a five-star hotel. I was touched that he was willing to ever give it up to play with us.

Curious to hear what Zhang Yong sounded like in such a

different context, I dragged a friend along to hear him at the glistening hotel in Beijing's new financial district, which had risen atop the rubble of a working-class neighborhood. The band played four nights a week on a large raised stage behind a gleaming bar. They were performing with polish and a lack of boredom that was impressive since there were only a handful of people in the bar, all of them couples composed of cute young Chinese women and big-bellied, middle-aged Western men. The place seemed to exist solely to provide a place for these mismatched pairs to have a drink before heading to their rooms.

The music was far more appealing. Everyone, including Zhang Yong, took turns singing songs by Coldplay, Lynyrd Skynyrd, and Steve Miller in perfect English, though none could speak the language. That was fascinating, but the biggest revelation was that Zhang Yong was a great singer, though he had never opened his mouth onstage with us.

ON MY WAY out of the hotel, I waited for the elevator with a European businessman about my age and his young companion. I looked at the floor and up at the ceiling as they cuddled and giggled. When my car came first, I stepped in and turned back, locking eyes with the man. He held my gaze, and neither of us betrayed our thoughts before the door closed and carried me away. This was a side of expat life in China that I often heard about but had really never experienced firsthand, having avoided the bars that catered to this crowd. This was a line I would never cross, and I found these Mr. Big Shots strolling around with Chinese girls on their arm quite absurd.

We really need more rehearsal. Please tell me what day this week we can meet.

Woodie's text was adamant and his message was clear: we had a lot to work on. When we spoke, he said that he had been embarrassed by our Jianghu debut, which shocked me. Evidently, my magical night had been his sloppy, unformed performance in front of musician friends. In two weeks we would debut at Yugong Yishan, Beijing's most prominent rock club, and he insisted that we work some things out.

We returned to the same basement studio, and Woodie was ready with new arrangements that turned my simple, lazy takes on blues standards into real songs. We had dramatic new beginnings and endings, pauses, stop rhythms, a capella sections, and harmony choruses.

Buoyed by how quickly this all came together, I showed the guys a half-formed song I had written sitting at a picnic table at Hong Kong Disney waiting for my kids to exit Space Mountain for the tenth time. When a chorus popped into my head, I grabbed a pen and jotted lyrics down on the side of a park map, then sang a few lines into my phone.

Back home I hammered out the shell of "I Don't Care," a song featuring a cool turnaround riff I struggled to play. Zhang Yong quickly simplified and improved it, and Lu Wei added tricky drum fills at the end of every verse. Just like that, my simple sketch had grown into a compelling funk blues. I had written dozens of half songs over the years, but had never had the push to complete them.

If our rehearsals could remain this productive, maybe we'd actually live up to the lofty slogan I had written for new posters a friend had designed for us: "Beijing's premier blues and jam band."

. . . .

YUGONG YISHAN WAS a huge step up from where we had been performing. The club held about six hundred and had a large stage and sound system and an impressive light show. As soon as we took the stage and hit our first chords, my nervousness receded and I fell into the groove, which carried me through two solid sets. Afterward Dave and I slapped each other on the back, but Woodie had disappeared.

I found him twenty minutes later, wrapping up cables and unplugging his gear.

"We did it." I bent down and unplugged my amp.

"Yeah, it was really good." Woodie's tone belied his words, so I wasn't surprised by what he said next. "But something was missing, too, and I don't know what."

"Everything sounds a lot better with the rehearsal, but we also lost some of the spontaneity and excitement that people responded to," I said.

I felt certain this was a developmental stage and that we could regain the spark by just playing more shows. But I could tell that he didn't really know what I meant, so I tried to clarify.

"We tightened everything up and now we have to loosen it back up."

I inherently understood that tight but loose was the key to everything, but it was a difficult concept to explain. I was just going to have to show Woodie and the other guys what I meant.

I MET MY Chinese bandmates for dinner at a Uighur restaurant around the corner from Jianghu Jiuba, the little club I loved. The Uighurs are ethnically Turkic people from China's Xinjiang Province in the far west, bordering Kazakhstan,

Pakistan, and other Central Asian nations. Their hearty, uniquely spiced cuisine also sits on the border of the Mideast and China. We ordered several dozen *chuar*—spiced barbecue meat on a stick—and shared wide, flat handmade noodles topped with a tangy tomato sauce and a huge plate of spicy chicken stew, which sat atop a giant disc of thick, crusty bread. We plowed through the stew, which had huge chunks of nutlike spices floating in it, and broke off the bread, dripping with the delicious broth. I ordered a few large bottles of Tsingtao but Woodie asked for a Coke.

"I stopped drinking," he said. "My doctor said I had a health problem and had to stop.

"That's why I have been unhappy the last few shows. It's the first time I have played without a drink and it's hard. I hear every mistake and obsess about each one. It feels like a job instead of a party and I get so upset that I can't enjoy myself."

"I think it will get easier," I said, choosing my words carefully.

Zhang Yong and Lu Wei were eating away, seemingly oblivious to what we were discussing, as I wondered what else I didn't know about my friend. I assumed that the doctor's story was a cover and that Woodie was telling me he was an alcoholic. What he said about struggling to play sober mirrored what many musicians, including Bonnie Raitt, had told me in interviews for *Guitar World*. I followed up with them, probing for more information and a deeper explanation, but I took a different approach with Woodie.

I thought there was a big difference between interviewing someone for a magazine article and talking to a friend. I respected the boundaries he was setting and tried not to pry. Asking questions and being a good listener were essential skills for being a good journalist, but I never wanted my friends to feel like they were my subjects. I was particularly sensitive to this in Beijing, where several people had admitted that they felt self-conscious around me, worried that something they said or did might end up in a column. I never wrote about anyone without their permission, but sensitivity to this issue may have heightened my reluctance to push Woodie for more information.

I did tell him how often I had heard similar stories, and how guitarist Jimmie Vaughan had related virtually the same tale about his little brother, Stevie Ray—the fiery guitarist whose face graced Woodie's arm. I wanted him to know that his heroes had wrestled with the same demons and proved that they could be vanquished, but I treaded carefully.

The part of Woodie's struggle that was clearly relevant to me was that he had channeled his anxiety into something very productive for the band; he had arranged those songs and driven us to rehearse them. That prompted me to finish writing a song, which we were already playing to applause. Maybe this change in Woodie's lifestyle would be good for all of us.

A COUPLE OF hours after dinner, we took the stage at Jianghu Jiuba in front of a packed crowd celebrating the great little club's first anniversary. We welcomed a steady stream of guests to the stage, including Tianxiao, who played tenor sax; three different harmonica players; and five guitarists, including shredder Powell Young.

We took a short break and as we returned to the stage, Woodie was excited. "Hang Tian, a really famous singer, is here," he said. "He quit performing but said he wants to sing. Let's call him up before he changes his mind."

Woodie introduced him, the crowd roared, and a professorial guy with a wispy beard, a tweed jacket, and long hair pulled back behind his ears shuffled up to the stage with a little wave.

Woodie looked at me and said: "E major shuffle." We laid down a hard-charging rhythm and Hang Tian started singing "Hey Hey Guniang" (basically "Hey There Ladies"), a Chinese jump blues that had the whole place singing along. When Hang Tian forgot the lyrics everyone else seemed to know, Zhang Yong, who had been singing harmony, took over lead vocals. I marveled again at his singing voice.

Hang Tian began the blues standard "Stormy Monday" before forgetting the lyrics and holding the mic up for me to finish the song. He walked off to applause, and we played the rest of the set without any guests, as everything we had been working toward came together. We were embodying the musical ideals I sought in everything I listened to: tight but loose.

We caught a groove and rode it hard for an hour. People were running in from the back room to see who was onstage. We were the great band in the hole in the wall that I had spent my life searching for. Something changed during that show; I saw a vision of what we could become, instead of just being happy with what we were. I thought I had been overly ambitious about the band, but now I realized that I had not been ambitious enough.

Nobody considered Woodie Alan a silly diversion anymore. Becky wouldn't complain about the gigs again. We both understood that this had outgrown my dreams and I had to see just how far I could take it.

# CHAPTER 21

# TEACH YOUR CHILDREN

"THIS. IS. BORING!"

To make sure I got her point, Anna flung herself up and landed hard back on my lap. We were jammed into the backseat of a cab with Jacob and Eli by our sides cruising through Shanghai's fetching French Concession in search of a park. Becky, seated in the front, looked back and we exchanged a meaningful stare conveying concern, consternation, and confusion.

We were wondering how our pint-size adrenaline junkie was not finding enough stimulation on this outing. We both would have struggled to combine the words *Shanghai*, *French Concession*, and *boring* in a meaningful sentence. After two and a half years in China, we were still not jaded by our surroundings.

But this life was normal for our kids: Beijing was where they lived, Shanghai was just another place to jump on a train and visit, and our vacations were consistently fantastic. Their expectations seemed awfully high after a couple of years living like this.

We had traveled to Shanghai with several other families and attended one megaevent after another: the huge Special Olympics opening ceremony, where Yao Ming waved at them; a fabulous acrobatics circus; and the Women's World Cup soccer finals, where we sat with the families of the American team. Each was a thrilling spectacle, making this little jaunt through the French Concession seem kind of lame, at least to Anna.

The moment encapsulated a concern I had since moving to China—that we were training our kids to expect too much with our new, internationally fabulous lifestyle, which included both frequent travel and a day-to-day existence that was far more grandiose than our lives back in the United States. Our fake rich lifestyle included daily household help, the gated community, regularly hiring drivers, and a general sense that access to anything was just a phone call away. I worried that this would warp their values and perspectives and instill a sense of entitlement—a trait for which Rebecca and I had little patience. I had already heard seven-year-old Eli and his friends discussing the relative merits of Thai and Malaysian beaches.

Becky and I struggled to make sure our kids felt the same sense of wonder we did every time we stepped off a train or plane in Asia. Sometimes it seemed to take hold—they grasped the wonder of feeding sea eagles in a Malaysian mangrove river and riding elephants through a Thai jungle. Other times they whined or begged to play Game Boys on the bus rather than visiting a Tibetan temple or taking in a stunning Sichuan mountain vista.

I was confident that the travel had at least opened my kids' minds as it had mine, helping them understand that the world is huge and interconnected, with an endless choice of places to go and people to meet. They were developing a far broader, more international outlook than I had as a child. I just didn't want them to think it was normal to bang around from one fancy Asian resort to another.

The easy solution would have been to slow down our traveling, but we were hell-bent on making the most of our time in Asia. We tried to balance the luxurious vacations with trips into rural Chinese places like Guizhou and western Sichuan. When we were first contemplating whether to move to Beijing, Becky pointed out that we had reached a stage in life where we were unlikely to undertake a lot of ambitious travel. "We can go see China and these places now or wait until we're retired in twenty-five years," she said.

I wrote a column on being worried about spoiling the kids that struck a nerve, flooding me with e-mail responses and even prompting NPR to interview me about my concerns. I was feeling good about myself, confident that I had tapped into a deeper truth about raising kids abroad.

Then I got a dose of reality.

When the column actually hit, we were on our way back to China from a Christmas-break visit to the United States, and the children were pouting on the plane. Even as I worried about them becoming pampered by fancy private schools, household help, and Asian beach vacations, they were longing for aging public schools, cleaning up after themselves, and trips to the Jersey Shore. My kids were starting to miss home and with each visit back to the States it became more difficult for them to accept the fact that they lived in China and we had no plans to move back soon.

When this job opportunity came up for Rebecca, we both understood that the timing was perfect to make an international move and that it would only get more difficult as our kids approached adolescence. Now Jacob was a veritable tween and was becoming more aware of what he was missing out on, realizing that life elsewhere didn't stop while we were on our adventure. Every time Jacob had had to say good-bye to someone, he gave them a big weepy hug and said, "See you in a year."

He was literally pained every time he bid farewell to a beloved cousin, developing a toothache whenever such a parting loomed. His mental state continued to affect his senses upon our return. We were groggily waiting in the passport line in Beijing when Jacob started complaining about extreme thirst. He walked to the water cooler, only to return spitting and gasping. "The water in China tastes horrible!" he said. We bought a Diet Coke on our way out the door and he reacted the same way. He was clearly sick about returning to China, and everything he put in his mouth reinforced the feeling. On the way home, he said he had to throw up twice and got out of the car, where he spit on the ground. All the while, he was muttering about "living on a different continent than everyone else."

Despite this wrenching reentry, he and Eli settled back into their old routines within a few days. Jacob's best friend, Kerk, who lived across the street, got a new puppy, and the three boys spent hours rolling around on the ground laughing as the dog licked their faces. Their simple delight reminded me how young they still were, no matter how adolescent Jacob sometimes acted.

He was nearing the end of the simple stage Anna was still enmeshed in—a phase of childhood where you really only need a stable home and your parents nearby to be happy anywhere in the world.

Jacob loved almost everything about living in China, but he was old enough and smart enough to begin understanding that he was also giving something up. Even as he settled into life as an international citizen, the transitions back and forth became more wrenching each time we visited the United States.

I thought my children were in an interesting position: we

had gone back frequently enough for them to maintain close relationships with their nine first cousins and several dear friends, and to maintain strongly American identities. And yet we lived in China.

I was just beginning to realize that there was a phrase for children raised overseas: Third Culture Kids (TCK). As David Pollock and Ruth Van Reken explained in their definitive book, *Third Culture Kids*, these children come from one culture, move with their parents to another, and end up feeling like they don't quite belong to either. Instead, they create a "third culture" and can most closely relate to others growing up in similar situations.

Before moving to Beijing I never realized how alienating the question "Where are you from?" could be. I had since met many families with children who held two or three passports from countries where they had never resided.

I was fascinated by this whole world, which had been right under my nose since we arrived in Expat Land, but which I was just learning about. The more I read up on it and talked to experts in the field, the more intrigued I became with the realization that our kids were betwixt and between. They would probably not be overseas long enough, or quite old enough, to fully become TCKs, and yet were perhaps too removed from daily life back home to be fully American.

As I sat alone at the kitchen table surfing the Internet and reading up on TCKs, Jacob walked downstairs, said he was thirsty, and asked if we still had "that Diet Coke from the airport." Happy to learn it was still in the refrigerator, he went over, poured himself a glass, and took a long drink. I never thought it could feel so good to watch one of my kids drink soda. The same bottle that had tasted poisonous to him upon arrival in Beijing now quenched his thirst and seemed to soothe his soul.

# CHAPTER 22

# THE HOUSE IS ROCKING

The band began meeting regularly at our new rehearsal space, a studio inside Lu Wei's duplex apartment in Tongzhou, on Beijing's eastern fringes. To get there from my place, you drove out of town, through some countryside, then reemerged in a sea of high-rises. It was a reminder of just how sprawled out Beijing was.

With over one million residents, Tongzhou felt like a separate city, one few foreigners in Beijing even knew existed. The first time I went there, I hired a driver; the second time a friend who speaks excellent Chinese accompanied me and spoke to Lu Wei all the way. After that, I drove myself, feeling proud every time I arrived at my drummer's run-down compound.

It looked like it had been built as a scaled-down version of Riviera but had never taken off. Weeds grew through the cracks in the asphalt, and many of the units were unoccupied. The raggedy young guards waved at me as I drove by.

As distant as the place felt, Lu Wei's house was immediately recognizable as a slacker band crash pad. I could have been in Ann Arbor or Austin. A couple of roommates lounged on a little couch in the middle of the day watching soap operas with their girlfriends. A small drying rack sat in the living room hung with laundry, including a pair of leopard-spotted panties. An overflowing ashtray sat on the coffee table, and a stack of Chinese drum, bass, and guitar magazines sat atop the rickety upstairs toilet.

One bedroom on the second floor had been converted into a studio, with a big sound system, nice monitors, and multiple microphones. Here we transformed Woodie Alan into a real band, ironing out the details of six new songs and transforming "Beijing Blues" into a true composition, which quickly became our theme song. Dave, busy with a real job, missed most of the rehearsals, marveling at the way we showed up for each gig with a new song or arrangement to show him.

We had played Hang Tian's "Hey Hey Guniang" at every gig since we learned it and I loved the song. Wanting to feature more Chinese singing, I translated verses from "Beijing Blues" and "Come to the Edge," a new song I had written, and told Zhang Yong that I wanted to try alternating verses in English and Chinese. He took the lyrics with him, but told Woodie that he did not want to do this. He had his own song he wanted to perform instead, and at our next rehearsal he picked up my acoustic guitar and played "Wo de Baobei" ("My Baby").

It was blues based but with a catchy pop essence and a depth that dwarfed its simple, poetic declaration of love—"You're my treasured love and always will be." We rehearsed it for an hour, debuted it the next week, and played it at every subsequent show.

Adding "Wo de Baobei" turned out to be the smartest thing we ever did, and not just because it made us a truly bicultural band. It also completely altered our relationship with Zhang

Yong. At thirty-five, he was a musical giant who could make any stringed instrument sing and had been playing professionally for sixteen years. Woodie Alan had been another in a long list of gigs, but now he had an ownership stake. He had written "Wo de Baobei" twelve years earlier, but this was the first time anyone wanted him to sing it.

Becky fell in love with the song the first time she heard it, moved by the melody, Zhang's impassioned vocals, and the unspoken power of having a mixed Chinese/American band perform a great Chinese love song. She joked that if "Wo de Baobei" ever hit the American airwaves, it could help repair U.S.–China relations. Our combination of expats and locals had always been unique, but it became much more pronounced as Zhang Yong stepped to the fore, making it clear that the band was not just a foreigner frontman with hired gun Chinese musicians. We were a true collaboration, which was essential to my understanding of what it took to be a real band.

I OFFERED ZHANG Yong a lift home one night after a late rehearsal. As I started up my van, the sound of prime Allman Brothers boomed through the stereo. I always loved the sensation of blaring über-American music while driving through China and had been listening to a vintage recording at high volume on my way there.

Zhang Yong's face lit up when he heard "In Memory of Elizabeth Reed," a monumental instrumental penned by guitarist Dickey Betts, whom I had interviewed many times.

"This is the Allman Brothers," I said in Mandarin. "Do you know them?"

"No, but I like," he replied in halting English. We listened without speaking for few minutes as the music washed over us—utterly familiar to me, amazingly fresh and foreign to him, even though it was almost forty years old.

"Two drums?" he asked.

"*Dui.*" (Correct.)

"Two lead guitars?"

"*Dui.*"

I clicked ahead to "You Don't Love Me," an original take on a traditional blues song, with Gregg Allman's whiskeyed blues vocals leading into inventive guitar soloing. Zhang was listening intently, astounded by what he was hearing.

Next up was the sweet, country-tinged "Blue Sky," with Betts's high, lonesome vocals leading into one of my favorite guitar solo sections in all of rock, as Betts and Duane Allman take flight separately before swooping back down to hit heavenly harmonies. Zhang Yong turned to me, grinning madly.

"Wow. Good! Different band?"

"*Bu shi! Yi yangde!*" (No, the same!)

"Oh wow. Two singers!"

We listened without speaking for a while, then he simply said, "Oh, so good."

It would be unthinkable to come across an American rocker of Zhang Yong's age and talent who did not know the Allman Brothers' music, which had so permeated classic rock radio. Turning him on to it felt fantastic. My musical connections with my Chinese bandmates had been so easy and complete that I had forgotten about the vast differences in our backgrounds.

No wonder I had not been able to quite communicate what I wanted or explain what I meant by "staying tight but loosening up." I was trying to describe the Allmans' music. It was grounded in the blues and built around perfectly executed riffs and licks, but the solos headed off on wild rambles, always managing to parachute right back onto the riff. That was the kind of approach I wanted us to take.

I burned three CDs of my favorite Allman Brothers tracks and handed them out at our next gig. A week later, Zhang Yong came to rehearsal and started playing and singing "Statesboro Blues," one of the Allmans' best-known songs, written eighty years earlier by Georgia bluesman Blind Willie McTell.

"He wants to do this song," Woodie said.

"Statesboro Blues" made the transition from 1928 Georgia to 2008 Beijing with ease, and we worked it up as a duet with Zhang Yong singing the first two verses and me taking the last two. Woodie also immersed himself in the Allmans' music, altering his entire conception of what he could do with the lap steel guitar. "I need to take it further," he said. "Now I hear all the possibilities of the instrument."

Woodie was inspired by the Allmans' young guitarist Derek Trucks, whom I knew well, having written many stories about him, starting when he was a twelve-year-old prodigy. Seeing Trucks perform with Eric Clapton in Shanghai had inspired me to want to play with Woodie, who was now being inspired by his brilliant playing. And the Allman Brothers, who had ignited my love for music, were now inspiring my Chinese bandmates. There was some sort of poetry at work here.

# CHAPTER 23

# YOU AIN'T GOING NOWHERE

One of the strange things about living somewhere for a defined time is the constant sense of a clock ticking away in the background. For us, this was not merely metaphorical. Those large clocks counting down the days until the August 8, 2008, opening ceremony of the Beijing Olympic Games were also targeting our scheduled departure. My relationship with the giant digital displays changed considerably over the years.

When we first saw the clock at Tiananmen Square, the thousand-plus remaining days made us feel like our time in China was limitless. That was both exciting and terrifying. Midway through our second year I saw the number "499" and was surprised to realize that our stay was more than half over. Returning from our summer visit home to begin our third year, I noted that the number was 348 and was forced to acknowledge that we had less than a year to go.

I watched the number grow smaller with increasing alarm, thinking about all the things left undone. It felt like the clock was mocking me. Want to see the Silk Road? Only 320 days left. Still want to make it to Japan? You better get busy—289 days until you leave. Think your band is going to play those cool Chinese festivals? 240 days to make it happen.

I remembered a conversation I had with Kathy Chen shortly after arriving. Entering her final year and possessing the long view, she was already envisioning the end of our assignment. "Before you know it, you'll be asking for an extension," she said.

What seemed like a ridiculous statement as we were trying to get our feet on the ground was now a prophecy coming true. Becky and I had been discussing extending for months, and I began pushing her to finalize a deal.

"Should we stay or should we go?" was a common expat conundrum, and I knew people spanning the entire range, from counting the days until they returned home to proudly having open time horizons. Some of these long-termers wanted to remain on expat packages for as long as possible, enjoying perks like subsidized private school education, while others had started businesses or otherwise become too entwined in local life to contemplate leaving even when this meant leaving corporate packages behind. Others just loved the daily adventure of living abroad, which had the tinge of perpetual vacation, since even the tough days tended to be interesting. Some people truly feared repatriating to a home country from which they had grown distant.

We were in the middle of this spectrum, sure we were returning but in no hurry to leave. I was no longer baffled by people with no exit strategy, or planning on moving on in an apparently endless stream of foreign postings, but neither option was really for us. We were too attached to our families. And we were undeniably, thoroughly American, which I no longer took for granted.

Though I had far more affinity for both life in China and the expat existence than I anticipated, my big-picture thoughts on returning to New Jersey had not changed. Our stay would not be open-ended, and we were unlikely to move on to another country. This strengthened my desire to extend—why hurry back from a life we were enjoying so much?

Becky was unsure of the career impact of so much time away from the home office, but I urged her to think about what she really wanted after a career spent being a good soldier. She was conflicted; as much as she loved our Beijing life, she had some reservations about extending.

We had told our families, including our children, that we would be gone for three years and she thought we should honor that pledge. My father's illness had also truly spooked Rebecca, and she dreaded the thought of enduring a repeat performance from afar. All four of our parents were doing just fine, but every month we stayed in Beijing was pushing our luck. This was true, I said, but a far too defensive mind-set.

Becky was also concerned about maintaining our torrid pace for another year. We were burning it on every front, working hard and playing hard. Her job was pressure packed and she was working more intensely than ever—which was saying a lot. This was normal for Asia-based Western expats who were on duty 24/7, with the home office checking in just as the Chinese day began winding down. When the kids went to sleep at 9:00 p.m. and she should have been kicking back after a long workday, people in New York were just starting to fire up their computers and wonder what was happening in China.

Becky often sat in our home office until the wee hours working with editors in New York to shape stories for the next day's paper. All-nighters were not uncommon, and she always slept with one eye open and her BlackBerry nearby. There was always something happening somewhere in China, and it was her responsibility to be on top of it.

It was difficult to separate my own desire to stay from my honest opinions about what would be best for Becky, but I truly believed that she would be leaving too soon. After building the bureau into a smooth-running, Pulitzer Prize–winning operation, it didn't seem right to just hand it over and walk away to a new challenge. She loved living in China, and I thought that she should just enjoy it without feeling guilty about reneging on an agreement that I had never considered binding.

I knew that extending would only mean kicking the moment of truth down the road for a year, but we simply weren't ready to leave. After debating the pros and cons, Rebecca asked for and received approval to extend from her bosses in New York. Now she had to make up her mind. With our tenant's lease on our Maplewood house up for renewal, our moment of truth arrived—we had our deadline, something we both always respected and met. After all the angst, the final decision was easy; the long process had allowed Becky to work through it and commit with a clear mind. We would be staying in Beijing for another year.

We had prepped our kids about the possibility, and they took it in stride, immediately asking which of their friends would remain through the next school year. That was the way expats thought. Eli was alarmed at some of his looming losses, but we tried to turn the conversation around to those who would stay.

I NEVER COULD have made a long-term commitment to living in China, however, because of the pollution, which could be mind-bendingly bad. Rapid economic growth spurred massive construction and an explosion in car ownership, overwhelming other improvements and keeping the air a thick stew of particles and pollutants.

We always knew what we were getting into; a few days into our look-see visit, the skies became hazy and the air began to smell. The "fog" grew for two days until we couldn't see the high-rise construction project outside our hotel-room window.

"It's good that you're seeing this," our guide said. "The pollution's not like this all the time but it does happen regularly and you should know that."

We were too excited to pause and really contemplate the potential health effects on our whole family. That lack of attention sometimes seemed foolish. I often saw a brown mist hovering above the city when I flew into Beijing, even on days that were crisp and blue on the ground. Many people complained about a "Beijing cough" that lingered for weeks. If we didn't ride our bikes for a few days, we would find them covered in dust and dirt. The school kept kids indoors on particularly bad pollution days, and Eli looked outside one nasty day and said, "Aw, today's not going to be any fun. It's too foggy to play outside."

Spring sandstorms were also regular occurrences, sometimes mixing with light precipitation to rain mud from the sky. It didn't rain actual water for our first eight months in Beijing until the sky opened for a thirty-hour drenching that evoked Noah. It felt like a rebirth afterward, with everything looking and smelling fresh and clean. The city had taken a shower, washing away a heavy layer of grime. I stepped out onto our third-floor balcony and stared dumbfounded at mountains gleaming on the horizon, visible for the first time. A sunset-painted sky reflected off ranges to the north and west, creating a vastly different landscape.

After a couple of atrocious pollution days, a friend told me that she had heard of someone finding out that their lungs had been damaged by years of living in Beijing. "Living here is like smoking a pack of cigarettes a day, you know," she said.

That sounded like an urban legend, but I couldn't shake the thought, so I asked my radiologist father-in-law to take a chest x-ray on our next visit. The good news was that my lungs looked perfectly normal. The bad news was that they would have looked the same if I actually had started smoking a pack a day two years prior.

"Smoking causes cumulative damage and it probably wouldn't show up in that short a time," he said.

There was no way to measure the damage that breathing in Beijing had done to any of us, but there was certainly reason to worry. The Asian Development Bank released statistics showing that Beijing had the dirtiest air of all major Asian cities, with a pollution level seven times higher than what the World Health Organization had deemed safe. I could sometimes feel the pollution in my lungs and in my eyes, as my contacts fogged up.

I spoke to an American environmental expert based in Beijing who said simply, "When it looks really bad outside, it's really bad." Still, she urged me to not overthink the problem, insisting that the air was no worse than it had been in the United States or Europe forty years earlier.

"Air pollution is a real problem here, but I think it's a disproportionate expat concern compared to all the other risks they take every day," she said.

She was talking about driving, which was a valid point, except that driving was optional, and breathing was not. Toward the end of my first year I had a persistent cold that became a hacking cough that lingered for weeks and had me expectorating huge gobs. I finally went to the hospital, where I saw a hip, good-looking Indonesian Australian doctor with an earring and nicely groomed, pointy sideburns.

He looked concerned listening to my chest. "Do you have a history of asthma?"

"No."

"Well, your breathing is very asthmatic. It's quite distinct. Are you short of breath?"

"A little."

"But you can exert yourself?"

"Yes, I went to the gym today."

"OK, good. Your lungs sound like you would get out of breath climbing a flight of stairs."

"Uh, do I have asthma now?"

"Probably not, though it is quite common for people who have never been asthmatic to become so in Beijing due to the atrocious air quality. Most likely, your cold has become a bacterial infection in your lungs and possibly your sinuses as well, causing restrictive airway disease—temporary asthma. I am giving you antibiotics, and I think you should have a Ventolin inhaler in case your breathing becomes more labored."

As he wrote the prescriptions, he told me that he had only been in Beijing for three months and that it had reinvigorated his passion for medicine.

"How so?"

"I was in private practice in Sydney for fifteen years and getting a little bored. You see the same things over and over. Then I came here and started seeing all these fascinating cases—things you only read about in case studies or see once a career back home."

"Really? Like what?"

"Oh, lots of things—TB, malaria, lots of pulmonary emboli, even medieval stuff like leprosy."

"You've had leprosy in this hospital?"

"Oh, yeah."

"You know what, Doctor, I don't want to hear any more about what you see here."

He laughed and we shook hands. The next day I was running around the soccer field encouraging kids at high volume and gasping for breath. I took several puffs of the inhaler, though I had never had respiratory issues before.

Still, I never really worried about myself—but my kids did not have a choice about where they lived, and we had just committed them to another year of sucking in Beijing air. They had actually been unusually healthy since arriving, with few of the normal colds and flus that strike most houses every year, but I was concerned.

Their pediatrician, Dr. Alan Mease, told me that the real issues and questions were all long term. "We just don't know what the effects will be when these kids are seventy or eighty," he said.

That was a scary thought, but I was mostly concerned about what it meant for the Chinese who would live and die there; our stay was going to be relatively brief with or without the extra year. Maybe that was just a rationalization. Maybe I would have come up with another one if the opportunity to stay in Beijing long term had presented itself. I was just happy to have that fourth year guaranteed.

# CHAPTER 24

# GIANT STEPS

I hoped that another year would be long enough for everything, including the band, to come to its logical conclusion. We were still on the rise. Woodie, finally confident that we were a "real band" with a growing repertoire of original tunes, had begun promoting us on Chinese-language websites and forums, which quickly paid off. A prominent music blog sent a reporter and photographer to interview me at Yugong Yishan for a feature on Woodie Alan, a name that lacked the humorous subtext to most Chinese but worked simply as "the Woodie and Alan Band."

As the opening act performed, I sat on a ratty couch in the dressing room behind the stage noodling on a guitar and talking to an eager, nervous young reporter as Woodie translated and Zhang Yong and Lu Wei listened in. It was my first interview from the other side of the recorder and answering questions felt a lot easier than asking them.

A few days later, a lengthy story about us appeared on the site, along with some great pictures from that show. It proclaimed us "Beijing's premier blues and jam band"—my

marketing ploy had worked. It also praised the way we inte-
grated Chinese and American songs and called attention to
our mix of expat and local musicians, which was unusual.

A photographer from *City Weekend*, one of two prominent
English-language magazines in town, was at the same gig, and
pictures of us ran in the next issue's gossip-y "Beijing Seen"
section. We were becoming acknowledged as stalwarts of Beijing's music scene, playing virtually every weekend in front of
crowds that were no longer dominated by our friends.

I enjoyed every gig, every rehearsal, every appearance in
a magazine, every band meal, and every time someone approached the bandstand after a show wanting to shake hands
or talk about music. I had grown used to being recognized
and becoming a semi-public figure because of my column, but
being known as a musician was different. I had been working
as a writer for my whole life and expected myself to produce
work that could touch people. Communicating some of the
same thoughts and feelings with music was more like a fantasy,
and I never ceased to appreciate the unlikely situation.

I began to feel like every show was our best one ever. I said
that walking offstage so many times over the next six months
that Woodie started laughing at me. But I was buoyed by this
constant sense of improvement, which pushed me to see how
much further we could go. The more a band plays together, the
more familiar with one another everyone grows and the easier
it becomes to take chances, confident that wherever you head,
your bandmates will be there waiting. Confidence that you can
steamroll over little errors encourages risk taking and allows
the music to pulse with life.

I understood all this intellectually, and as a listener I had
little use for groups that didn't take chances. But it was thrilling
to feel it happening *in my band*. I was beginning to think we

could achieve the high standard to which I held others. We were inching toward the elusive goal I had laid out for Woodie after that first Yugong gig: loosening up while retaining the tightness we had worked so hard to obtain.

One night, I brought the volume down low, trying to draw listeners in. Then I hit my strings hard and raised the volume of my voice. Lu Wei was right on top of my move, slamming his snare drum at precisely the right moment, creating a dramatic effect. I toyed with the dynamics for the rest of the song, hitting the strings harder and softer to see if Lu Wei would follow. He was right with me every time, and I knew that we had reached yet another peak. I felt like I was steering a freight train, with an incredible degree of control at my fingertips.

Our improvement was being noted, which became clear when I received e-mail notification that we had been nominated as Band of the Year in the *City Weekend* magazine reader's poll. I had to read the message three times and actually go see the online ballot before I could believe it was real. Our three competitors were all young, hip Chinese bands with record deals and European and American tours and profiles. I didn't think we had a chance to win, but having our name on the ballot was a great honor, which I immediately began trumpeting in promotional e-mails.

We had been talking about recording some original music for months and this honor pushed us to finally get going. Woodie booked a basement studio owned by one of China's best-known session guitarists to record five songs. Two days before the session, a *City Weekend* reporter called, asking to interview me for the Best of Beijing issue.

"Tell me how you all met and the keys to growing into Beijing's best band," he said.

"Wait a second. Did we actually win?"

"Yes, of course. I'm sorry. Someone was supposed to call you yesterday."

I restrained myself from screaming with joy and completed the interview in a state of amused amazement, with my heart beating rapidly. A cocktail of positive emotions swirled through me: I was proud, tickled, cracking up, and just basically blown away. As soon as I hung up, I dialed Woodie's number and waited impatiently through his Avril Lavigne ringtone.

"Hello, Mr. Paul," he answered. "How are you today?"

"We won, Woodie. We are *City Weekend* Band of the Year!"

"Ha ha. Wow. Congratulations, Alan. That's just . . . incredible. What an accomplishment."

We promised to celebrate the next day when we already had plans to meet for lunch and discuss the recording session. We entered the studio riding a high.

MODERN STUDIO RECORDING is a strange process quite antithetical to a jam-based band like ours. I eventually convinced Woodie and the guys to cut several songs live in a rehearsal space, but they insisted on beginning the process the tried-and-true modern way; recording each instrument separately, then layering them together afterward in a final mix. You start with drums, then add bass and rhythm guitar and finally vocals and solos.

It's a long, tedious job and after the initial rush of excitement died down, the day grew long and I was still hours from touching my guitar. My phone battery was dead, and I was uncomfortable being out of pocket from my family for so long. With nothing much to do, I drove home to check on the kids and make sure their homework got done.

I plugged my phone in, and it was immediately flooded with text messages. The most recent, from my friend Susan, read,

I hope Jacob's OK. That looked bad.

I called her immediately.

"What happened?" I tried to maintain my composure. "My phone was out."

"Jacob hurt his arm playing T-ball and it looks broken. He is with Wyatt."

I called Wyatt and learned that he and Jacob were on the way to the hospital, where Becky would meet them. Everybody had been frantically trying to call me.

"My phone was out," I said. "Is he okay?"

"He's calm and the arm is in a sling, but it's definitely broken. We will be at the hospital in a few minutes."

"I'll be there in twenty."

I arrived right after Rebecca, just as Jacob and Wyatt were walking out of the x-ray room. Jacob's skin was ash white, his right arm deep purple and hanging in front of him, his hand dangling at a grotesque angle, as if his wrist had moved three inches up his arm. I hugged him gently and kept my arm around him, guiding him back to the Emergency Room, his mother on the other side of him.

"It really hurts," he cried, finally letting down the brave front he had maintained with Wyatt. He calmed down after a shot of morphine and told me that he had gotten hurt diving into first base. "I was safe," he added.

Dr. Wang, a friendly, seventy-something orthopedic surgeon who had trained in the United States decades ago, spoke great English, and reminded me a bit of a Chinese Dixie Doc, came in and popped the x-ray into a viewer. It was obviously a bad break, both forearm bones snapped just shy of a compound fracture. We held Jacob's left hand as he was wheeled into the operating room to have his right arm set, kissing his forehead and waving good-bye just before the door swung shut behind his stretcher.

As Becky and I sat in the waiting room nervously awaiting news, I reflected on just how close I came to spending the night in the studio oblivious to what was happening to my son. This was a scary intersection of my two worlds.

WE PICKED UP our Band of the Year Award at a ceremony inside a half-built luxury mall, one of many similar structures around Beijing. We were asked to perform but Lu Wei and Zhang Yong were unavailable, with a commitment to another band, so Dave, Woodie, and I performed as a trio. Playing in the same minimal alignment with which we had debuted fourteen months earlier made it obvious just how far we had come.

Two willowy models handed us our award, which the three of us accepted with glee. In photos snapped a moment later, we are smiling ear to ear, holding the award plaque between us, our arms draped over one another's shoulders. Anything felt possible.

WE RESUMED RECORDING in a new studio in Lu Wei's remote neighborhood. It was inside a house tucked away in a quiet, dead-end alley, close to the last subway stop on Beijing's Eastern line. I learned the disadvantage of the remote locale when talk turned to dinner.

"The only place that will deliver here is a donkey burger restaurant," Woodie said.

"Are you serious?" I asked. "How about some fried noodles?"

"Sorry, but I guess it's donkey burgers or nothing. Will you try that? They're actually pretty good."

With my stomach growling, I agreed. I had been open to trying anything since I arrived in China, but I didn't really seek out exotic food adventures. Southern China was more famous for its eat-anything ethos, and I had skipped Beijing's famous penis restaurant and passed on a couple offers of dog. Now it looked like it was time to give donkey a try.

Dave soon arrived, wearing a suit, holding a sax in one hand and a briefcase in the other.

"Do we have any food?" he asked. "I'm starving."

"It's on the way and you're in for a treat," I said, with a laugh.

A few minutes later, the engineer walked in carrying a cardboard box stacked with little sandwiches on wax paper—barbecued donkey sliders. They were surprisingly good, tasting a lot like barbecued brisket on fresh focaccia. Westerners don't associate Chinese food with bread, but local Beijing cuisine has a wide range of tasty, freshly made rolls. After gobbling a couple down, I entered the studio and finally laid down vocals for my first two songs.

It was strange singing in a quiet room all by myself, listening to the music on big headphones. In this sterile environment, it was hard to attain the same level of emotional involvement and intensity I reached onstage, but I did not feel nervous.

Dave played parts until after 1:00 a.m., then Lu Wei called us a driver. As we stood on the street waiting for him to find us, Dave was furiously pecking at his BlackBerry, as he often did until moments before we took the stage, sometimes taking orders from the treasury secretary. As the U.S. Treasury Department representative in Beijing, his job was to meet with Chinese officials and explain official U.S. economic policy.

Now the financial crisis was exploding and he was in the middle of the fire. I realized how little I knew about what he had to deal with as I watched him standing in this remote outpost of Beijing in the middle of the night intensely discussing complex issues of vital importance to the world economy. We were friends and neighbors. We shared many meals with our wives. Our sons played together and ran in and out of each other's houses without a thought. No one else had shared the experience of being Americans in Woodie Alan. Yet we had rarely discussed his job or our internal lives. We shared an intimacy that seemed to transcend the need to talk about anything much.

The driver finally showed up, we climbed into the white subcompact car, and I offered directions to Riviera. We pulled into the silent, dark compound after a traffic-free half-hour drive, with the car shaking and shimmying anytime he pushed it past 50 miles per hour. I cranked down the window and told the guard who stopped us my house number. He smiled at me—the guards always seemed amused by my rolling home in the middle of the night in all sorts of vehicles—and opened the gate. As we pulled in, the driver whistled at the sight of the huge, dark houses and laughed. "You guys are rich!" he said in Chinese. I laughed nervously. I really had nothing to say to this.

The next day, when Woodie and I returned alone to the studio to finish our vocal and guitar tracks, I brought along some instant coffee and snacks. We had almost finished recording five original songs and were well on our way to having an album done.

# CHAPTER 25

# COME AND GO BLUES

June is the cruelest month in Expat Land. The transient community undergoes an annual end-of-school turnover that never really gets any easier. Each member of our family lost a dear friend every year, often a soulmate without whom Beijing was unimaginable.

By our third year, I had adopted an attitude reminiscent of my grandmother's perspective on outliving most of her friends. As we celebrated her eighty-fifth birthday, she told me, "After a while when you hear the news, you think, 'What a pity. Thank God it's not me.'"

*What a pity. Thank God it's not me.*

That's exactly how it felt every time my band took the stage at a farewell party and launched into Bob Dylan's "You're Gonna Make Me Lonesome When You Go." This song had become my signature way of saying good-bye while also morphing into a Woodie Alan centerpiece. We had completely rewritten the music, with an extended introduction featuring Zhang Yong's distinctly Asian solo, making the piece our most successful East/West hybrid. It felt more original to me than the eight songs we had written and played every night.

Resetting our own clock to stay for another year lifted a burden from our shoulders, but it didn't alter anyone else's time frame. We were saying good-bye to some stalwart friends whose companionship had marked our time in Beijing.

Eli was particularly devastated that the Camerons were leaving; their son, Race, had been like a brother since we arrived in Beijing, and their house was his second home. Their departure only reinforced his view of expat living as an endless series of heartbreaks, a perspective formed when a great friend left for Singapore a year earlier.

"We are stuck," he said as the two of us drove home from a friend's house one afternoon. "Wherever we are now, we'll be away from people we want to be with."

"You can't look at it that way," I said. "Everyone in America is still there and we still love them and they still love us. And now you also have all these great new friends. After we go back to America, we'll have friends in Australia, Hong Kong, China, England. . . ."

This was a kids' version of "it's better to have loved and lost than never to have loved at all," and he saw through it as clearly as everyone else nursing a broken heart always has.

"No," he insisted. "We were fine before, but now we'll always feel sad about someone not being close to us."

I couldn't really disagree with him. We were knee-deep in planning farewell parties for two couples, both of whom we would miss dearly. I thought we would discuss these events over a dinner of Hou Ayi's gong bao chicken and sautéed greens, but Becky had something else on her mind. The paper wanted her to return to New York to become the international news editor. The fact that this was the precise job I had just recently suggested would be an ideal post-China gig only made the news harder to digest. I couldn't really resist, but they wanted her back in New York immediately, which was simply unacceptable.

Rebecca had always been an extremely loyal company sol-ider, but I suggested that maybe it was time to step out of char-acter and flex some of those Pulitzer muscles. Wrapped up in our friends' impending departures, it was unfathomable that we too might soon be packing up our house.

Though Becky had struggled with the decision to extend, she had felt a great sense of relief and never looked back once it was finalized. She wasn't ready to leave and felt horribly guilty about the prospect of suddenly uprooting the family and espe-cially me from a life she knew I loved.

The Olympics also presented a major logistical hurdle. They were just six weeks away and we were both credentialed to work the Games. The Olympics had loomed over our entire stay in Beijing and leaving before them was unthinkable. I had worked for years to get a gig as an NBC.com blogger, while Becky was not only covering the Games, but also overseeing logistics for the *Journal*'s entire team.

Leaving just after the Olympics was also problematic, since by then school would be on the verge of starting in New Jersey. When she told her bosses that she couldn't possibly leave before the school term ended in December, she thought she had put them off without quite saying no.

They called her bluff, however, by saying that she could start in January. There were a lot of details to work out, and she dragged her feet in formally accepting the job, but leaving early now seemed inevitable.

As much as I wanted to stay longer, I never suggested that Rebecca turn down the job, because it was clearly perfect for her. I got a lot of credit for moving around the world for my wife's job and I was not above basking in it, but I never lost sight of the fact that her success had opened this door and would inevitably close it as well.

All corporate expats serve at someone else's pleasure. Our little community was rife with people being yanked around like yo-yos by the invisible hand of the home office. I watched friends live with tremendous uncertainty, unsure until the final days of their contract whether they would be renewed for another year and, if not, where they would be headed. We were being granted the opportunity for a civilized departure.

But being intellectually understanding did not mean that I was not emotionally roiled. I knew how fast the time would fly. We were in the middle of a steady stream of visitors, which would end with Jacob and Eli returning to the United States to spend three weeks with relatives as Becky and I worked twelve- to fifteen-hour days throughout the Olympics. By the time the kids returned, we'd have four fast-moving months left.

THE IDEA OF leaving Beijing now heightened every sensation. It made me treasure every moment and every experience and begin looking at everything with new eyes and renewed interest. This is the state I was in when I got an e-mail from Kristi Belete, who had recently moved, asking me to go over to their house and pick up a few things they had left behind. Walking into their emptied house shook me up. All signs of their vibrant household were gone, and I recoiled when a management rep asked if I was the new tenant. The very idea of someone else moving in to my friends' house offended me.

That empty building reminded me why stuff didn't really matter: we make the inanimate objects come to life. My expat experience had largely liberated me from an attachment to specific places and things. I thought leaving our house in New Jersey would be difficult, but I had rarely thought about it. I had no idea what was in the container of belongings we had left in storage and knew that I wouldn't have missed anything if it all just vanished.

Walking through Nathan and Kristi's former house searching for their missing items, I was also overcome by the realization of the extent to which my fond feelings for Beijing and the Riv were wrapped up in the people. There was no charm to these bare walls, studded with hooks where pictures of a vibrant, smiling family used to hang. The friends I loved were gone and this was just a structure now. I began to contemplate what for me had been unthinkable: how all this would look when I was gone.

We wanted to wait until we were certain about the move before telling the kids. But it was impossible to put it off any longer because too many people were beginning to discuss it and we didn't want them to hear secondhand. We kept everyone in the kitchen after dinner one night and told the kids that it looked like we'd be heading back to New Jersey in December, at the end of the fall semester, instead of July.

Anna burst into tears. She didn't remember living anywhere other than China. Her only memories of Maplewood were our visits home, and she lacked the great friends there that her brothers had retained.

Eli pumped his fist and only had one question: "Is it for certain?"

He had been counting down the days until our departure from China for the last year, ever since that trip to D.C. Once, when we told the kids that they could each pick one thing to buy at the massive Panjiayuan Flea Market, packed with

Chinese knickknacks, Eli found an American-flag-clad *Apollo* moon landing glass. I feared that he had idealized America and his life there.

"It's not going to be like when we visit," I reminded him. "You are going to go to school and have homework and everyone isn't going to rush over to see us every day."

"I know," he insisted. "That's fine."

Jacob had the most complicated, nuanced reaction, both because he was the oldest and because he truly had mixed emotions. He understood not only what he was gaining—all those cousins he struggled to say good-bye to—but also what he was giving up. As hard as it had been for him to return from our last trips to the United States, he loved almost everything about living in China.

He loved the regular trips to the Great Wall; the beautiful, fascinating parks teeming with people; the travel; the baked sweet potatoes bought for a dime from migrants pedaling around with giant, coal-heated oil drums on the back of their bikes; his British school and its sports teams; and his terrific crew of international friends. Leaving it all behind was going to be difficult and he knew it.

IN THE MIDST of all this turmoil, my parents arrived for their second visit, joined by Aunt Joan and Uncle Ben and my brother's son Jesse, who would spend the summer with us. These kinds of visits were always a mix of great fun and high stress, as we felt pressure to keep everyone entertained. We used a tour guide to escort visitors to Beijing sights, but I also loved taking visitors to my favorite spots.

My dad joined Woodie Alan for two gigs, as we transformed ourselves into a Dixieland band for a few songs. The

Chinese guys enjoyed the change of pace and the opportunity to meet my father, whom they treated with great respect. He was equally impressed with them.

"These guys are really good," he said, sitting on the patio of the Stone Boat, just before he was to join us for our second set. My father was famous for carrying his horn with him everywhere, ready to jump on any stage, but now he hesitated, though the previous night's performance had gone well.

"You sound so good I don't want to break your groove," he said. "These guys are wonderful musicians and I am really impressed by the whole thing, in a way I just didn't get from watching the YouTube videos. I'm sorry that I didn't take it more seriously. I see now that you have something really great happening here."

I insisted that he join us. My father's blessing meant a lot, and we all had fun faking our way through jazz standards like "All of Me" and "When the Saints Go Marching In." Afterward, with my family long gone, I sat on the porch with Woodie and Jonathan, eating peanuts and sipping beer and tea. I had planned to tell Woodie that I was probably leaving in six months, but I just couldn't do it. I wanted to savor this moment, not spoil it.

THE NEXT MORNING, the sweetness turned sour. Over coffee, I corrected my dad when he said something about "when we returned" to the United States in December.

"*If* we return in December," I said. "It's not final yet."

"Oh, come on. Why are you resisting the obvious? You've had your fun. Now it's time to get back to reality."

The comment hung in the air for a moment before I responded.

"*Reality?*" The word stung me and stuck in my throat. It just sounded so wrong. "Did you say, 'Get back to reality'?"

"Yes, and your brother agrees, by the way."

I did not actually care what either of them thought, and I found his comment deeply offensive. I rejected the implication that I was playing around, that this incredible life we had crafted was a mere illusion, a dream we must awaken from. I understood that all the domestic help allowed us to live a fake rich lifestyle, and I had seen people become addicted to its trappings. But the real advantage was simply more time to do interesting, fun, and productive things.

One of the lessons I had taken from expat life was that no one was destined to live by any single reality. There were a million different possibilities, and no one could convince me our life wasn't real. I had never done more than I did now or felt more alive. The key for me was figuring out how to maintain this vibrancy in the looming new reality.

I could accept that it was probably time to leave and understood why. I would never block Becky's career path nor resent her for the very thing that had made this whole venture possible. But I would not *celebrate* what was happening, and I would never marginalize my expat life. It was a wonderful reality.

# CHAPTER 26

# MOUNTAIN HIGH, RIVER DEEP

I didn't tell anyone else about my dispute with my father. A few weeks later I would mention his comment in a column without saying who uttered it. That prompted my father to call to apologize and many readers to e-mail me with their own similar stories; "time to get back to reality" turned out to be a phrase expats heard all the time.

But I kept all this to myself at first; I was tense enough wrestling with my emotions while leading everyone on a tour of interior China that involved two overnight train rides in three days. This spectacularly poor planning reflected the pitfalls of trying to do too many things at once.

I wore a lot of hats in China: father, husband, columnist, musician, blogger, Olympics reporter, and employer. But tour guide was probably the most challenging and anxiety provoking. I always wanted visiting family and friends to have not only a great time, but a genuine "China experience." I wanted to take them off the tourist track and let them experience China as we did.

The problem was, when people say they want to go off the beaten track, you never know just how deep into the weeds they really want to head. And in China it's not hard to fall into a rut and end up in a dangerous or difficult situation. A year before, we had taken Becky's parents, aunt, and sister on a beautiful but harrowing bus trip through Sichuan's mountainous west, climbing over sixteen-thousand-foot passes on torn-up roads with no guardrails teetering over thousand-foot cliffs. Alone with a guide in a four-by-four it would have been the greatest trip I ever took, but it was sheer insanity in an oversized coach bus with a party of nine ranging in age from four to sixty-nine. I was alternately terrified, furious at the guides who had led us to the precipice, and wallowing in guilt over planning the trip. Only everyone's good humor and my mother-in-law's ability to tell hour-long versions of common fairy tales kept us sane.

THIS TIME I tried to play it safer, with a trip to the ancient walled city of Pingyao and Xi'an, home of the famous terra-cotta warriors, which was close to Huashan, the holy mountain where Yechen now lived and that I planned to visit. I relied on a travel agent I had used many times to plan the trip even though I had long ago learned the pitfalls of trusting the sensibilities of a Chinese guide or agent. They tended to emphasize seeing as much as possible over lingering in any one place. This trip ran away from me and it was too late to change by the time I realized we were booked onto two twelve-hour train rides in three nights.

I had underestimated the distance between the two cities and overlooked the fact that the wonderful trips we had taken on overnight trains between Beijing and Shanghai had been on China's newest, fanciest line. There were some significant differences this time—which didn't bother our kids at all and wouldn't have bothered us, either, except that I was viewing everything through my guests' eyes. Times like this made me realize how much my own perspective had changed. Things that seemed normal to us were anything but for our visitors, who had never eaten a donkey burger or covered their mouths with bandannas as they shut their eyes and squatted in a fetid village outhouse.

There are four classes of Chinese train tickets—hard seat, soft seat, hard sleeper, and soft sleeper. We had always taken the latter, which features cabins with four bunks and privacy, as well as bathrooms used by fewer people. Many stations also have special soft-ticket waiting areas, but not the massive Beijing West Railway Station. We walked into a giant room packed with migrant workers heading home laden down with huge bags. A toddler in split-back pants peed on the floor a few feet away from us. Because the hard-seat cars are unreserved—and many people have to stand for days to get to their destinations—the line for the train formed early, already snaking to the back of the room an hour before departure.

There was a huge surge when the train was called, with people pushing and shoving as one great mass. We let it settle down a bit before joining the scrum. Walking onto the platform, I saw that our train was decades older than anything we had ridden before. We trudged along, looking up at people piling into the hard sleepers, which are lined with bunks stacked to the ceiling.

"This train looks like it dates back to Chiang Kai-shek," my astounded father said, referring to the defeated Nationalist leader who left for Taiwan in 1950.

The day before, my travel agent had called with the bad news that our party of ten could only get seven soft-sleeper tickets—split among three cabins—and three hard sleepers. As we boarded and the reality of being scattered across two cars bunking with strangers set in, I began to feel anxious, guilty, and rather incompetent. Everyone else was enjoying the madness, however.

All ten of us crowded into a cabin, the adults cracking open a bottle of wine while the kids climbed to the top bunks, happily settling into a vivid game of make-believe. Jacob's arm was in a brace that had replaced his cast. We toasted our trip and laughed at the situation. I was already anticipating the next problem; how was my mother, who struggled with squat toilets, going to relieve herself for the next twelve hours?

Most Chinese bathrooms have one Western-style toilet, marked "For Deformed Man (or Woman) Only." I set out to ask the conductor if the train was similarly equipped. She didn't understand my request, so I searched my Chinese vocabulary and cobbled together a sentence.

"My mother is very old and her health is very bad. She can't use the regular toilets and needs a special one."

Understanding flashed through the conductor's eyes and she leaped out of her seat and jogged to the other end of the car, where she unlocked a door, revealing a clean Western-style toilet. I thanked her profusely and escorted my mother to my discovery.

"Welcome to your private bathroom," I said.

Later, my mother went for a walk and the same conductor who unlocked the bathroom ran up to Rebecca. "The old lady is walking alone!" she exclaimed. "Is that OK?"

In the middle of the night, with the toilet's door locked, my mother sought help from the conductor with the aid of valiant Uncle Ben, who found the entire train crew eating noodles in the dining car and somehow managed to pantomime "deformed woman restroom." Worried that the conductor would notice that she was anything but infirm, my very fit, exercise-crazy mother hunched her back and dragged her foot behind her in an approximation of a disabled woman.

I couldn't assist her myself because Rebecca, seven-year-old Eli, and I had decamped for a hard sleeper, where my son and I slept soundly next to each other on top bunks, twelve feet off the ground, in an open cabin with almost seventy fellow passengers. Rebecca slept directly below Eli, across from a loudly snoring man. As foreigners, we had caused a small stir when we entered the car.

While most of the passengers were sleeping, I climbed down from my perch and went for a late-night stroll. I bought a beer and walked to the far end of the dining car, where I stopped in my tracks. I looked through the window of the back door, across the small connector and into the next car, which was full of hard seats—the cheapest class. People were jammed in shoulder-to-shoulder, flank-to-flank. I made eye contact with several young women, who betrayed no emotion but made me embarrassed about fretting over our own conditions.

I woke up at 5:30 and climbed down to look out the window and sip tea next to an old man doing the same while the rest of the cabin snoozed. Eli and Rebecca were the last people sleeping—I had to rouse both of them as we neared our destination at 7:00 a.m.

We spent two low-key days in dusty, picturesque Pingyao, which is a world historical site because it is a rare example of a preserved walled Chinese city. Most walls were torn down in the 1950s and 1960s as relics of a feudal past.

Then Becky returned to Beijing to work, and I was on my own as guide on our second overnight train ride. This time we had two soft-sleeper berths and the car was newer, but it stopped everywhere, making for an interminable trip. Staring out at a tiny station in the middle of Shanxi Province, I realized with a start that I had forgotten to let Yechen know I was heading his way. I sent my old teacher a text.

I'm very sorry for the late notice but I will be at Huashan in
two days and I hope I can see you.

I was thrilled when my phone beeped with his response
shortly after I arrived in Xi'an.

I am here and happy to see you. Let me know when you are
coming.

In Xi'an, we climbed onto a minibus for a long day touring
around the warriors. I returned to the hotel late that afternoon
soaked in sweat, exhausted, and a bit beaten down from a long,
hot day of touring on the heels of another night on a train. As
I walked off the elevator, my phone rang. It was Becky, back
in Beijing, and I answered trying to sound more chipper than I
felt. Her own enthusiasm was clearly genuine.

"You won!"

"I won what?"

"*The columnist contest*. A letter came to New York and the
secretary sent it here and I just opened it. You are columnist of
the year!"

It took me a few seconds to process this information, which
my wife was spilling out in an excited rush. A WSJ editor in
New York had submitted my column months ago for an award
with the National Society of Newspaper Columnists and we
had chosen three entries. I had forgotten all about it until now.
This was incredible news, especially at a moment where I had
lost sight of the big picture and was feeling a bit sorry for myself.

"Congratulations," Becky said. "I am so proud of you and
wish I could be with you to celebrate. Go mark this event and
we'll have champagne when you get back."

The wave we had been riding since day one just kept getting

higher, and I looked forward to marking the moment with Becky. She had always been somewhat uncomfortable with my writing about our personal lives, so I felt like I owed her an extra thank-you for letting down her guard and giving me her blessing to document our lives. Most of all I owed her thanks for getting us over here in the first place.

The rest of us celebrated over dinner at a remarkable restaurant, which served endless rounds of different dumplings, stuffed with everything from pumpkin to fried rice. It felt right to mark another China-based success with a delicious version of the country's traditional good luck comfort food. I only wished Becky was there to share the meal.

I WAS STILL buzzing the next day as we climbed back onto the minibus for the hour-long drive to Huashan. We rode to a gondola station, where I was to meet Yechen. My mother took the kids for a walk, buying them fake Pringles, while I sat on a hard bench in the hot sun, looking up at the spectacular peaks looming above us and waiting for my friend.

Fifteen minutes later, two monks walked slowly up the hill. I rose to greet my old teacher, who did not look well, with pale skin and sunken eyes. He had lost weight and seemed to have aged ten years in the few months since I saw him when he visited Beijing.

A smile briefly lit up his face when he saw me. I wanted to hug him, but he only offered a limp handshake. I introduced him to my crew, and we all walked over to the cable car together. As we waited in line, I told him of the near certainty that I would be returning to the United States in less than six months. He showed little emotion but said he hoped I could return to Huashan alone for a longer visit before leaving China.

Huashan is an imposing mountain. The hike is famous for its

difficulty and danger; every year people die on the treacherous walkways, which in many places host two-way traffic on wooden beams suspended from sheer cliffs by hanging chains. Yechen, though not physically strong, had made the hike many times. As we soared up in a cable car, he pointed down to show me the trail and tell me how much he would like me to hike it with him.

The gondola ride was nerve-racking. The cable rose straight up a large peak, before dropping down the other side, descending in hair-raising fashion before turning back up and depositing us at the 5,290-foot North Peak. The mountain has four other peaks, soaring up to seven thousand feet, and a series of trails. Yechen wanted me to accompany him up to some high-altitude temples, far beyond what my parents or kids would or should attempt.

I explained this to him and said that although my time was limited, I would like to venture out a bit. Jacob accompanied us as we left the others behind.

"This is my best friend," Yechen said as we ascended, pointing to his fellow monk. "He has really helped me. He's very nice, but there are a lot of fake monks, even here."

Yechen was a purist and an idealist and had really thought that he would find a like-minded community at Huashan, only to be disappointed once again. Few could meet his exacting standards; he found even the monks at one of Taoism's most sacred places lacking.

At the temple, another monk offered us seats on tiny stools as well as sweet white peaches and tasty green tea. Yechen taught Jacob how to bow and pray properly, and we both got to our knees and prostrated ourselves before a graven image. It was a nice moment even if, as Jacob later noted, we were breaking one of the Ten Commandments. Although I could feel Yechen's excitement in showing all this to me, I knew that he was not doing well. I was trying to decide how hard to dig, but he made the decision easy by opening up as we descended a set of steep steps.

"I often go days without leaving my room," he whispered. "I just read, write, and sleep."

*Textbook depression symptoms*, I thought.

He continued. "I lost myself, you know. I have no more self-confidence."

He not only looked to me like he was fading away; he felt that way about himself, too. I asked him what his mother thought, and he said that she still did not know where he was—this was why he had kept the same cell-phone number, which had allowed me to find him. She had been growing increasingly worried, knowing that something was not right.

"She called me crying the other day," he said. "The night before she had a dream that I had vanished."

"In a way she's right."

I was not going to hold back what I thought. No one had ever said anything this direct to me about the precariousness of his or her mental state and I had to respond in a similarly forthright manner. I had been haunted by my failure to offer smarter, more concrete advice when he sought my counsel a year ago, and I would not make the same mistake again. I knew this was probably the last time I would see him for a very long time.

Yechen had been such an important early guide to China. Now I was riding high while he seemed to be sinking fast. The dichotomy was jarring, hard to accept and impossible to understand. How had I found myself in China while this native son was losing himself? How could I pull him out of his hole?

I looked back and saw Jacob a few steps behind, holding hands with Yechen's friend, who was helping him down the steep stone steps.

"You need to think about things. If this is not the right place for you, then you need to move on. That does not make you a failure. It just means you tried something and it didn't work out. It means this is another part of your journey, not your final place. That's fine. You will be a better, smarter, richer person for having had this experience."

Yechen nodded in agreement, but I wasn't sure he was truly listening. We had stopped climbing and were standing atop a giant rock. Jacob and his friend were behind us looking out over the spectacular landscape.

"You have to understand that sometimes the journey is more important than the destination," I said.

It felt strange to be offering him the same kind of aphorism-laden advice he used to give me, but I was trying to be honest and caring. I told him that he was always welcome to stay with us in Beijing, and that if he wanted to look for jobs abroad again, I would help him do so. "You can always e-mail or call me," I said. "I'll help you any way I can."

He thanked me, but I doubted he would follow up. Yechen walked us back to the gondola and said he wouldn't be joining us on the ride down. He wanted to head higher up the mountain to visit more temples. Jacob said good-bye, and I turned back to Yechen.

"It was very good to see you," I said. "I think of you all the time and miss you. Please be in touch."

He thanked me for my friendship and my concern and assured me he would be fine. "Keep practicing your Chinese," he said. "It sounds good."

He gave me a heartier handshake than he had at the bottom, and I said good-bye and put my arm around Jacob's shoulder as we headed down a steep walkway on the final descent to the cable car. Just before entering the station, I looked back and saw the two monks walking back up the mountain.

# CHAPTER 27

# BEIJING BLUES

I still had not told Woodie about the growing likelihood that I would be leaving early and it was beginning to feel like a burden. I went to several gigs intending to talk about it but just couldn't do so. Even thinking about it was excruciating, and not just because of how Woodie might react. It would also force me to confront the impact moving would have on *me*. It would force me to say aloud and acknowledge that this was happening, and what it meant for Woodie Alan.

We had put so much into building the band and still felt very much like we were on our way up. Contemplating its end was too much to bear, and I could feel myself immersing into the music more deeply at each show. As every performance gained a new poignancy, I entered a virtual trance state, completely focused on the music to the exclusion of anything else.

My time of reckoning—of discussing this with Woodie—was drawing near because I was working on a column that I planned to publish as soon as we officially made the decision to leave. After another great Jianghu show, this one featuring a guest appearance by my visiting brother on guitar, Woodie and I sat in the courtyard on a beautiful warm night. I just blurted out my news.

"It looks like we are probably moving back in December." After holding this information inside for so long, it felt good just to get it out, but Woodie looked at me blankly, stunned by my words.

"What? Why?"

"Becky got a new job and is being moved back."

I lamely filled the silence that hung between us.

"They wanted us to go back now but I said we couldn't."

Woodie took the news stoically, not saying much, but it was not his way to reveal his true feelings. I knew that we were both hurting and feared that he and especially Lu Wei and Zhang Yong might see the band as a sinking ship and start looking for other opportunities.

"Look," I said to him. "I still have six months here and I am not giving up on this band. And I really hope that no one else does either."

A week later, we played a gig at Cheers, a small bar in the city's sleazy Sanlitun bar district, which was crawling with disreputable characters of every nationality. The area had oddly been ignored in the city's pre-Olympics security crackdown, which had halted performances at many bars, including the Stone Boat.

Onstage in front of a room packed with partyers of every race, I lost myself in the music, pulling the crowd in even as I paid them no mind. I was in it for myself, not entertaining anyone. It felt like I had crossed a threshold, vanquishing any remaining inhibitions. On the slow blues "Hold On to What You've Got," I dug so hard into my solo that it felt like I might push a string through the fretboard, and I sang Johnny Copeland's lyrics with a raw intensity and naked emotion that surprised even me.

*You've got to hold on / Hold on what you've got . . .*
*You know the grass might look greener way over on*
*the other side / but you better believe me when I tell*
*you, that just might be the devil in disguise.*

These lines were clearly written about romantic love and the temptations of adultery, but my emotions led me to a very different reading. Were we releasing our grip on something wonderful for the lure of the devil in disguise? That fear enlivened everything I did. I suddenly felt like a man on borrowed time, and I threw myself into life with heightened intensity.

After the show, I walked out into the hallway to talk to Woodie. Lu Wei and Zhang Yong were looking at me oddly.

"I told them about you leaving," a subdued Woodie said. "They are really shocked and sad."

We were standing in a cramped landing atop a staircase. Cheers was on the middle floor of a building hosting several rowdy bars. Drunken Westerners spilled up and down the stairs, drinks in hand, smoking cigarettes, chasing skirts, talking loudly. I didn't know what to say. I looked at Lu Wei and Zhang Yong and sort of shrugged and smirked, a half-assed way of communicating, "I'm sorry. There's nothing I can do. I hate it, too."

"Please," I told Woodie, "tell them that I am not giving up on the band and I do not want them to, either."

"It's not a problem, Alan," Woodie said. "These guys are not going anywhere."

The next day, he sent me a text message: Your singing was fantastic last night.

Thanks, I wrote back. It felt like something happened. I went to another place. I don't know how else to explain it but I'm glad you heard it, too. It wasn't just in my head.

Definitely not. What happened is now you've got the blues! Write a song about it, man!

There was something to what Woodie was saying. I had reached a new level of connection to my emotions, which were running hot and deep. But there was something else, also: faced with the reality that this would not last forever, that it could end too soon, I was determined not to leave anything on the table. I had always held back a small part of myself, because letting it all go and laying yourself bare makes you vulnerable. It can be scary out there, but my only remaining fear was regret—that I would get back and know that I could have done this a little better.

I did not have a lot of vocal range. I could barely sing "Happy Birthday" in tune. But I could connect with people emotionally by singing with soul—singing as if I had no choice but to sing—and I was going to do it every time Woodie Alan took the stage.

# CHAPTER 28

# GAMES PEOPLE PLAY

The Olympics were looming from the day we arrived in Beijing. Anticipation of the Games was so omnipresent for so long that it sometimes seemed they would never actually happen. During our entire stay, "the Olympics" was the answer to any question about any development anywhere in Beijing, two simple words that explained why anything was happening. Then, overnight, the Games crossed some invisible line from distant metaphor to real event.

On July 1, 2008, Olympics traffic lanes appeared on the Airport Expressway. English-language signs sprouted all over the city, directing visitors to hotels, venues, press centers, and tourist attractions. Blue-shirted volunteers were everywhere, ready to answer anyone's questions in Chinese or English. The monorail to the massive new airport terminal ran right by the Riviera, with empty cars flying by on test runs. The planting spree that had turned the side of Beijing's busy roads into verdant green space continued, with huge teams planting shrubbery at busy intersections.

The Riv, too, had embraced the Olympics spirit, suddenly

festooned with flags representing various sports, with the back entrance bearing giant letters spelling out the Olympics slogan, "One World, One Dream" in English on the right side, Chinese on the left. Across from the front entrance, a huge lawn decoration, at least twenty-five square feet, read "Beijing 2008" below giant Olympics rings.

Patriotism surged, with cars now flying small Chinese flags. Vendors all over the city were selling Chinese, American, German, British, and Australian flags, which were popping up all over Riviera.

I was hired as a full-time NBC employee for three weeks, and I got lost when I tried to find the International Broadcast Center (IBC), in the heart of the sprawling Olympics Green, for the first time. That was fitting, because my three years compiling an insider's knowledge of Beijing were often useless during the Olympics, which actually didn't take place in Beijing, but in Olympics land. It was an entirely separate universe whose heart was the twenty-eight-hundred-acre Greens.

A taxi dropped me off at a security checkpoint at the farthest point away from the IBC. Late for a meeting and hustling along under a hot sun I decided to hitch a ride on the next vehicle that appeared. That was a garbage truck. The two friendly drivers were amused by my plight and delighted that I could speak Chinese. I showed them the IBC on a map and they nodded and rumbled off. They delivered me to the front door, where I thanked them before hopping down to join the stream of journalists disembarking from a bus.

For the next sixteen days I was wrapped up in a parallel universe, alternating between two worlds as I covered events while also reporting on the Games' impact in Beijing. Rebecca and I crossed paths a few times, covering the same event for the first time in our careers— unbelievably, it was women's weight lifting.

Bands around Beijing were also busy, after months spent trying to line up shows during the Games. With no way to know what my schedule would be, I booked three high-paying corporate events and kept my fingers crossed, rushing to them from events at the soaring landmark Bird's Nest Stadium. Twice, the other guys played an instrumental set while waiting for me to arrive.

The last gig was a black-tie hotel ballroom soiree for the British Olympics committee, featuring several gold medal winners and a who's who of British business bigwigs. We were all dressed in new black suits—the first such clothes Lu Wei and Zhang Yong had ever owned. When I handed Zhang Yong his share of our $2,500 payday, he smiled and thanked me, with a look of awe.

"This is the most money he's ever made for a gig in sixteen years of performing," Woodie explained.

I was very happy to have made that happen.

For the closing ceremony, I was back in the streets, reporting on how the event was being viewed in Beijing. I strolled through old hutong neighborhoods and watched parts of the ceremony on TVs in restaurants and in little corner shops. The whole city felt like a party waiting to happen, but with nowhere to go. Huge TVs in public squares were black; the government had decided not to host public viewings, apparently concerned about large gatherings.

Late at night, I got in a car and headed across town and heard huge explosions coming from behind me. Looking in the rearview mirror, I saw fireworks fill the sky. I told the driver to pull over. I climbed out, joining hundreds of people standing in the lanes of a normally busy road, blocking a highway on-ramp. More residents emerged from the surrounding neighborhood to get a good view of the official closing of the 2008 Olympic Games.

The fireworks went on and on, the longest, most elaborate display I have ever seen. "Beautiful!" exclaimed someone in the crowd. "The best!" said another. A guy to my left turned to me and said, simply and accurately, in Mandarin, "Chinese people have the best fireworks."

The acrid smell of gunpowder filled the air as a massive series of colorful explosions signaled the grand finale.

And then it was over. The smoke hovered and drifted in curlicues and clouds as the crowd began drifting back to their neighborhood and traffic resumed pulsing by. I thought about a few parties I had been invited to, before telling the driver my home address. *Enough already*, I thought. I had to file a final post to NBC.com's Destination Beijing blog and then post-Olympics life in Beijing would commence.

I had outlived the clocks. Now my real countdown had begun.

# CHAPTER 29

# BIG IN CHINA

I had envisioned the moment when the digital countdown clocks turned off as a time to relax and enjoy some valedictory time in China. But with just a few months left in Beijing, I went into a hyperactive state. I lived with a manic intensity that had me playing gigs every weekend, recording tracks at night, mounting two tours outside Beijing, traveling to India to visit relocated Beijing friends, and heading to Lhasa, Tibet, when the Chinese government suddenly granted us visas.

Woodie also had been busy, booking us all over China. First up was a trip to Xiamen, a southern port city that was the closest point on mainland China to Taiwan. We would headline the Beach Festival, held on the shore overlooking the Taiwan Straits. After two festival performances and one club gig there, we'd head to Changsha, the capital of Hunan, the home province of both Mao Zedong and Lu Wei. A chain of nightclubs celebrating their anniversary booked us into all three of their venues after searching online to find "Beijing's best band."

We left with a bag full of hastily pressed five-song CDs labeled "Beijing Blues Tour 2008" and flew to Xiamen together.

We were joined by Jacob, Dave's family, and three other Beijing bands, a veritable rock-and-roll circus. A festival rep met us at the airport and I felt a surge of excitement loading our gear into the minibus: we were a real band, on the road in China.

We climbed off the bus at the festival grounds, and I stared in awe at the giant stage on the beach, with the Taiwan Straits lapping onto the sand thirty yards behind. Rows of bleachers extended far down a boardwalk lined with food and crafts vendors and flanked by Corona beer concessions and giant sand castles. We were escorted to a giant poster featuring the names of all the performers, with "Woodie Alan" in three-foot-high letters. The promoter handed us markers and we signed as cameras whirled.

After a noodle dinner, we were escorted to seats in the front row of the roped-off VIP section to watch our openers, a hip-hop pop band with two young women singing in English and mugging for the cameras. A full moon lit up the beach, and just before we took the stage, hundreds of lanterns filled the air, sent aloft by candles creating little hot air balloons. They drifted up and out into the crashing surf, a haunting and beautiful scene.

Dave and I said good-bye to our families and rose to join the band on the side of the stage. As I walked away, Jacob called my name. I bent down to talk and he crooked his arm over my neck, pulling me close. "Good luck, Dad," he whispered in my ear.

We were used to being packed tight onto tiny stages, so it was disorienting to be spread widely across this giant space. When they placed my microphone several steps ahead of everyone else, I felt distinctly, profoundly alone. I had always avoided distinguishing myself from anyone in the band, but now the spotlight was being thrust on me.

I couldn't understand everything the MC said in his introduction, but I heard my name and caught this loud and clear: *"Beijing zui haode yuedue: Woodie Alan!"* (Beijing's best band: Woodie Alan!)

I stepped up to the mic and swallowed hard as the crowd of five thousand Xiamen residents cheered. I blinked into the blinding spotlight and cursed myself for tossing off my sunglasses just before walking out.

I offered up my Chinese introduction about music making us all one people, then nodded to Lu Wei, who kicked off the "Beijing Blues" beat. We wobbled off the ground but righted ourselves and began to soar. The Chinese songs, a novelty item in front of our expat crowds, drew these listeners in. I roamed the big stage egging Dave and Woodie on with their solos. Jacob leaned against the front of the stage filming with my camera and smiled at me, flanked by Dave's sons.

Most Americans thought that having a blues band with three Chinese guys sounded like a punch line, but this was no joke. Few Westerners seemed to even know that guys like my bandmates existed, because they were outside the normal China narrative. They were not migrant workers or struggling peasants. They were not political dissidents or corporate go-getters.

After three years in China, I was annoyed by how many Americans still believed one of two diametrically opposed stereotypes: China is a raging dragon about to gobble us up; China is a land of faceless peasant drones riding bikes in Mao jackets. The truth is, China is a huge, fast-changing, incredibly diverse place; there was no way to summarize it and I ran away from anyone who tried. There were bars and rock clubs outfitted with great sound systems and knowledgeable soundmen all through the country, and more and more events like the Beach Festival were being held, but it still all felt new and exciting to everyone, which lent these performances added energy and edge.

Pulling back into the hotel late at night I saw another side of China. The huge karaoke clubs that flanked our hotel had been stolid white buildings during the day but were now lit up with garish flashing neon. Cabs and private cars were lined up in front. The hotel lobby was filled with Chinese businessmen and heavily made-up, scantily clad working girls from the clubs waiting to get rooms.

THE LOEVINGERS RETURNED to Beijing with Jacob for the start of the workweek, and I was alone in Xiamen with my three Chinese bandmates. The next afternoon, Woodie and I set out to buy some tea. Fujian is a famous tea-growing province and I had been enjoying the local product, especially Tie Guan Yin, or Iron Buddha. As its name implied, this tea was strong but smooth, and I wanted to take some home.

We walked to a strip of tea shops, which are ubiquitous all over China and even more so in Xiamen. I headed for the closest, biggest one, but Woodie insisted we check them all out first. He zeroed in on a small shop where two young women sat at a round table picking stems out of tea leaves.

"Hello, little sister," he said, sitting down. One of my favorite things about the Chinese language was the extensive vocabulary delineating someone's precise relationship—"my father's oldest sister's second son"—and the way in which it was polite to call strangers by family names. A young woman could be "little sister" and an older man "dear uncle." Many young people had abandoned these traditional greetings, but Woodie embraced them, which I found charming.

We lingered over tiny cups of tea, which the clerks continuously refilled.

"This whole trip has been one of the highlights of my life," I said. "It was incredibly cool to have a giant Chinese crowd responding to our music like that."

"I was thinking about what this must mean to you and Dave . . . trying to imagine doing this in a different country."

"That gives it so much meaning, but the thing is, it never would have happened at home. This band has allowed me to discover something inside of me, something that I always hoped was there but was never sure about."

I took a sip and thought for a moment before continuing. "I owe you so much for helping me tap into that—for making this happen."

Woodie flicked his hands in a dismissive wave and shook his head. "You don't owe me anything. *You* made it happen. We did it together. And it means a lot to me, too."

I sipped my tea and thought about that. Woodie had played so many more gigs than I had, touring throughout China and Australia, that I couldn't believe that these performances had as much meaning for him.

"Why has this been so special to you?" I asked.

"It's the music in my heart," he said. "This is the first band that I really felt was mine. Other times I've been playing the parts that fit the music, or what someone else wanted to hear. This is the music that I love and when I play, it is coming from inside."

He paused, trying to gather his thoughts and express himself properly in English. "That's . . . well, it's just so different."

"It's the best, Woodie," I said. "I'm glad you pushed us, by arranging the songs and asking me to practice more."

"I really didn't think you'd say yes. You were so busy with so many things . . . the kids and everything."

"Yeah, but I always felt like this could be special; and when I realized you did, too, I wanted to go for it. Especially since when you said you wanted to talk about the band, I thought you were going to tell me you wanted to break it up."

Woodie howled with laughter. "No! I wouldn't have called a meeting to break up the band; I would have just stopped returning your phone calls and e-mails. But I always loved playing with you. From the first time you jammed with Sand, I took you seriously as a musician—not as an expat asshole showing off—because of the way you carried yourself."

"Wow," I said. "We should have talked more."

Woodie nodded, and we both sipped our Iron Buddha before I spoke again.

"Let's kick ass tonight. Full speed ahead."

I raised my little cup and we clinked in a toast to that evening's performance—and to finally talking about everything we had been living for the past year. For as much time as we had spent together and how important we had become to each other, Woodie and I had taken precious little time to just talk. And he was just getting started.

"I had a bad drinking problem, you know. That's why I quit."

I didn't tell him that I had always suspected as much, instead just sticking with the facts: "I never saw you drink too much."

"I was good at hiding it, but I would go home after our shows and keep drinking by myself. I lost my business, which was doing really well, because of my drinking and I finally had to face up to it and accept that I was an alcoholic and needed to stop."

Woodie's Purple Buzz guitar business had simply disappeared. One day he had it, the next he was working as a relocation consultant, shepherding expat executives around Beijing housing compounds and schools. He never explained what happened and I never pried. In many ways, Woodie was a closed book and I wasn't sure if not trying harder to open him up made me a very good friend or a very bad one.

"Do Zhang Yong and Lu Wei know that you were an alcoholic?"

"I *am* an alcoholic; it doesn't go away. They know that I drank too much—I did it way more in the other band, without you and Dave around. But we Chinese don't really have this concept of the alcoholic. I had to face up to it when an Australian friend sent me articles of tests to take and I clicked "yes" to everything and that made it obvious.

"I really struggled quitting and that's why some of the shows we played were so hard. I was falling back and forth and having a hard time learning how to make music sober, which I had never done before. I'm really happy I did it."

Our musical collaboration felt entirely intimate, and it seemed proper for our dialogue to finally be the same. Maybe we should have taken a trip outside of Beijing together a long time ago.


ZHANG YONG ALSO plays the guqin, a traditional seven-stringed Chinese instrument, and that night he and I opened our second festival performance with an improvised acoustic guitar/guqin duet. We were creating an East/West fusion on the fly. I walked onstage confident, absent of the nerves of the first night there, and was able to step outside myself. I could stop thinking and allow the music to flow effortlessly from the first note. I now took it for granted that everything would be fine and aimed higher, pushing it to be great. I was no longer embarrassed to be bold.

Back at the hotel, I moved right through the congregated businessmen and their dates for the night. I needed to rest; I was in the middle of an important business trip.

# CHAPTER 30

# BITTERSWEET SURRENDER

Lu Wei, our drummer, whipped out his phone and pushed a button. "Father," he exclaimed. "I am in Hunan!" We were still on the plane, pulling up to the gate in Changsha.

A native of the province, Lu Wei hadn't been home since he left for Beijing eight years earlier when his father told him not to come back until he was "a big success." Despite growing acclaim in Beijing and endorsement deals with two large European drum companies, he still did not feel ready to return. A third-generation drummer, Lu Wei dropped out of school at age thirteen to study with his father and had dedicated his life to music. I offered to buy a train ticket to have his father come see the shows, but he politely declined.

His hometown was on the other side of the province, a ten-hour drive away, and he had never been to Changsha. Still, Lu Wei felt like he was home, beaming as he reveled in the soulful, spicy food and insisting on ordering for the whole table every time we entered a restaurant, choosing frog's leg stew, sautéed beef, huge steamed rolls, fiery crayfish, and crisp strips of pork sautéed with black beans and peppers.

With Dave back in Beijing trying to keep the world economy on its axis, we were scheduled to perform as a four-piece. When the club owners objected, wanting us to sound "just like on the Internet," Woodie hired Tianxiao, the owner of the Jianghu bar who took the fifteen-hour train from Beijing, arriving with only his sax case. He didn't bring a single piece of clothing other than what was on his body.

Leaving for our first sound check, Lu Wei walked out of the elevator and into the hotel lobby trailed by a clean-cut, friendly young man. Carrying the drummer's cymbals, Lu Wei's friend bowed slightly toward me, said "Ni hao," and picked up my guitar. As the lone foreigner and the oldest member of the band, I was receiving priority service, but I had no idea who the kid was.

"He's a fan of Lu Wei's who has come to help him set up," Woodie explained, as we walked out to flag down a cab. "Basically, he's our roadie."

"How does Lu Wei have a fan who will be our roadie in Changsha?"

I thought this was astounding, but Woodie just shrugged. "He has a very popular website where he gives video drum lessons and advice in a forum. This kid is a drum student who really looks up to him."

We would go on to play in four other cities around China and at least one of these guys showed up every time. Back in Beijing, Lu Wei, who did not have a day job, also had a personal assistant, a driver, and several other young acolytes who followed him around. He would soon hire a manager to handle his endorsement deals and book him gigs with touring pop stars. We may have been the only band who did not have a manager, but whose drummer did.

Our first gig was at Coco's "private club for successful

people," a members-only establishment that looked like the bastard child of a 1970s fondue restaurant and a high-end brothel, with burnished wood and red banquettes everywhere. It also featured an impressively stocked cigar humidor and an extensive private bottle collection where members kept their own wine, cognac, and scotch.

The packed crowd cheered loudly before and after every song, a remarkably enthusiastic reception for American roots music in Chairman Mao's home province. Though it was a Wednesday night, people were partying hard.

When we kicked into our next-to-last song, "Hey Hey Guniang," the hard-charging Chinese jump blues sung by Zhang Yong, three beefy tough guys and their beautiful molls started dancing right in front of the stage. I had noted them all night as they alternated between drinking cognac in their banquette booth and leaping up to cheer. One of the men stumbled toward me, with something in his hand. I couldn't make out what it was until he stuck a giant Cuban cigar in my mouth and raised his lighter with an unsteady hand.

I continued to pound away on my guitar, the giant stogie protruding out of my crooked grin. My hand was aching and bleeding under the bandages from a cut I received from a broken beer bottle in Xiamen, but I didn't even notice. As we segued into the American jump blues "Kansas City," I held the cigar in my left hand and spread my arms wide as I belted out, "I'm going to Kansas City, Kansas City here I come." Watching all these Chinese people grow almost delirious, dancing with abandon, I growled out the lyrics:

*They got some crazy little women there and I'm*
*gonna get me one.*

When we ended the night with "Soulshine," the crowd clapped along, swaying to the music and waving lighters in the air. I thought of Warren Haynes, the Allman Brothers Band guitarist who wrote the song, and remembered all the time I had spent listening to his music, watching him play, and interviewing him on his tour bus and in his New York apartment. I imagined how happy he would be to have his music spread so far from home, and for the first time I understood the ecstasy of the evangelist. I felt like a preacher spreading the gospel into the farthest reaches of China.

When we finished playing, the tough who had given me the cigar pulled me down into his banquette and poured me a glass of Courvoisier. He and his buddies patted me on the back, as two long-legged beauties slid in on either side of me. When one of the thick-necked men raised his snifter in salute, I realized that the girls were just like the cigar and the cognac to them—rewards offered for a job well done.

Before I could sneak away, I felt a hand on each of my thighs. One of the women pulled me close and whispered into my ear, in slurred, drunken English.

"What is the name of your bass player?"

"Zhang Yong."

"If you bring me to Zhang Yong, you can touch me anywhere."

She squeezed my thigh hard. Then the other one pulled me to her and put her lips inside my ear. "Don't bring her to your bass player." She was equally drunk. "Bring *me*."

The first one yanked me back. "Touch me *any*where!"

I laughed at the fact that the first time I had groupies they were just trying to get to Zhang Yong, but I wasn't surprised. The quiet, self-possessed bassist had several beautiful girlfriends in Beijing, sometimes showing up at an afternoon gig with one and an evening performance with another. When I asked him once, in Chinese, how many girlfriends he had, he laughed and responded, in English, "Many, many girlfriends."

I just wanted to get away from both of these women. The path of least resistance was to lead the more persistent one to Zhang Yong, who could certainly handle her more easily than I could. "Just come with me," I said.

She slid out of the booth and rose onto unsteady feet. When I got up, she put her arm around my waist and leaned into my side. We walked into the back room where the band was sitting at a discreet corner table. Surprise washed over everyone's faces at the sight of this beautiful Chinese woman draped over me. "Don't worry," I said in Chinese. "She wants Zhang Yong."

He got up and laughed when I told him to be careful. They walked off together, and five minutes later he returned alone and said that he had walked outside and put her in a cab.

THE NEXT DAY, we did three radio interviews, performing live at each station. The last appearance was at the biggest station in town. The glass-enclosed studio sat high above the city's biggest intersection. The two female DJs were very professional, and in and out of commercial breaks they played a clip promoting our appearance. It featured "Beijing Blues" and "Wo de Baobei," with a loud classic radio voice intoning, in Chinese, "The Woodie Alan Band—Beijing's finest blues band. Live in Changsha. Right here on the *Live Show*!"

We answered a few question from listeners calling in and played another song live, then sat listening to "Beijing Blues" booming through the studio monitors. I turned to Woodie, sitting by my side. "Can you believe this?" I asked.

"I'm proud of us," he said, smiling. "Just really proud."

Woodie and I sat reveling in this exciting, unlikely moment, playing out exactly like a scene in a music biopic. Zhang Yong broke our reverie when he suddenly acknowledged the elephant in the room. "It's too bad you're leaving, Alan," he said in Chinese with a wry smile. "Look at us."

None of us had discussed my impending departure, though it hung over the entire week, lending everything added emotional intensity and bittersweet shading. The Xiamen promoters had offered an extensive tour of Fujian Province, and one of the radio hosts wanted to book us onto one of China's most popular television shows the next time we came to Changsha. We all knew that neither was likely to happen. This trip was instead going to be the beginning of the end of us as an everyday touring band.

ON OUR THIRD and final night in town, we sold out Coco's largest venue, packed with 350 people who paid 40 RMB (about $6) each to hear us. It felt like the shows on this tour had been our first ever in China, because there were only a handful of Westerners in the crowds. No one knew us or was there because we were their friends. Instead, they all had laid down money to be entertained, and I was proud to send them home satisfied.

We were getting better from playing so many shows and spending so much time together. Our performances were like conversations, becoming more intimate and cohesive and less predictable, even to us. We all listened intently to one another and filled in little gaps and aural white space, often with subtle prods that could send a song in another direction. I felt an increasing ability to connect with and pull any crowd into the music.

As Woodie started playing his extended intro solo that kicked off "Will the Circle Be Unbroken," I raised my hands over my head and started clapping. A chill ran down my spine when most of the crowd joined in. I was helping a roomful of Chinese people feel the power of a traditional American song of mourning and redemption.

Singing this music made me acutely aware of what being an American meant to me: a deep, personal freedom that had little to do with politics and everything to do with individuality. I knew that I never could have pulled this deeply held feeling out of myself without the prodding of these great Chinese musicians. That to me was the very definition of global harmony.

It also made me ponder my own relationship to the blues I loved so much. I had been so amazed to discover Woodie and his tattoo of Stevie Ray Vaughan. It seemed so exotic to have found a Chinese person who had been so deeply affected by this profoundly American music. And indeed it was an unlikely journey for Woodie from his hometown of Langfang, an hour south of Beijing, to being a thoroughly legitimate bluesman—a journey that began with late-night radio broadcasts and pirated cassette tapes purchased at a flea market. But what made my own situation any more probable?

I was the son of an upper-middle-class Jewish pediatrician from Pittsburgh. Woodie was the working-class son of a Chinese small-business owner. We had both been drawn to the blues, feeling a profound emotional connection to this music born of African American suffering and advanced by white southerners like Vaughan and the Allman Brothers. Woodie was twelve years younger than I, and both of us were born long after the music was truly contemporary, but nothing else touched either of us in remotely the same way.

The hold this music had on us was hard to explain; that it had drawn us together and bonded us like brothers was impossible to deny.

AFTER THE SHOW we had our fifth and final meal at the twenty-four-hour noodle restaurant that had become our Changsha home base. It was a humble place, serving a small variety of fresh, delicious noodles for less than two dollars a bowl. We supplemented the main dish with a variety of cold, marinated sides selected from a cart. The guys all grabbed little plates of cilantro-laden, pickled root vegetables, tripe, pigs' feet, and other things that tasted so good that I didn't want to know what they were.

It was 2:30 a.m. and a car was picking me up to take me to the airport in five hours. I would be back in time to coach Jacob's soccer game at noon. I was wiped out and needed sleep, but I would never skip one of these great postgig meals. Besides, I had a lot of questions. We had traveled an incredible distance in just a year together, yet had barely discussed any of it. My teatime conversation with Woodie left me wondering how the other guys felt about the band. I asked if they had heard my singing improve.

Zhang Yong shrugged. "To me, your singing was always good. You just lacked confidence. The thing that wasn't good enough at first was your guitar playing."

We all laughed. Lu Wei, smoking a cigarette, scolded Zhang Yong for speaking so bluntly, but I encouraged him. "I want to know. What about as a bandleader? Could you tell I hadn't done this before?"

"To me, you are just a man who loves music," Lu Wei said. "You are the best bandleader I have met."

That answer was so unexpected that I was rendered momentarily speechless as Lu Wei plowed ahead.

"The thing I really admire is you consider all possibilities on every issue. You taught me a new way to play."

I had not taught Lu Wei anything other than how to feel a blues rhythm and that was done strictly by encouragement and example. "You are a great drummer—a far better musician than me."

"That has nothing to do with it! There is more freedom playing with Woodie Alan than any other band, and I began to understand why this was such a good idea: the freedom encourages you to perform better. With you, my feeling of playing is different each performance—even performing the same music at the same place."

This was natural to me; I had no interest in playing the same songs the same way every time. But it was a revelation for Lu Wei.

"I love this kind of excitement," he said. "With other bands, I often feel like I'm just playing to complete the work. But it is quite different with Woodie Alan—every song has excitement, and I always feel highly emotional."

Woodie was translating and I was recording the whole fast-moving conversation on my phone, hoping it was capturing every word. Lu Wei was echoing back to me exactly what I thought all music—and even life itself—should be about: playing with emotion, following your gut instincts, retaining spontaneity while being in control, practiced, and professional.

Zhang Yong was nodding along with everything that Lu Wei said, occasionally adding his own amplifications.

"You are very tolerant," he said. "With you, we can do whatever we want to do because you are very willing to try different things and respect our thoughts. We feel really relaxed and enjoy the freedom. Most Chinese bandleaders just want everyone to follow his ideas.

"Our band is always in a good mood because everybody came to it for fun. We had no rules for rehearsal, and we all drink and eat together—like this. It means a lot."

I wondered what Woodie thought about all this, but when I asked, he looked at me like I was a slow child, unable to grasp that two plus two was four.

"I feel exactly the same."

When we finally rose to leave, Woodie said the three of them were going to get foot massages and urged me to join them. "There's no point sleeping now for you anyhow," he said.

He had a point but I needed to digest the conversation and write it down before the feeling was lost. My vision of my role in the band had been completely wrong. I thought that my relative inexperience rendered me the student, but I was also the teacher. I wondered if remaining oblivious about this had allowed me to blossom in the role without self-consciousness.

I thought about my former teacher. Maybe Yechen and I had more in common than I realized. He had thrived in London, where his attachment to an ancient Chinese way of life, which was out of step with contemporary China, was charming and even cutting edge. In my home culture, I had thrived around the margins of popular culture by being an expert on musicians and athletes far removed from their glory days. I had to come to China to be relevant to the contemporary conversation, and to truly reinvent and find myself.

# CHAPTER 31

# TICK TOCK

I biked home from a jaunt through a nearby village one morning, with thin plastic bags steamed up with fresh-baked scallion pancakes in my front basket. I was thinking about the ride, about the movers on their way to assess our house, and about those pancakes, which I was excited to get home and eat. I was not thinking about the short remaining ride as I turned the corner onto our circle at high speed and almost ran over my friend and neighbor Deirdre Smyth. Walking just inside the curb, she yelped as I slammed on my brakes and yanked the handlebar to the right, skidding to a halt just in front of her. She laughed as I apologized profusely.

"It's OK," she said, mock-slapping me across the face. "How's the move going?"

"Oh, it's fine. It's just exhausting and kind of hard to believe it's actually happening. The movers are coming in half an hour to start calculating."

A Venezuelan native, Deirdre was an expat lifer, who had moved to Beijing from Oman a year before we arrived and would leave for Moscow six months after we departed. She had seen hundreds of friends come and go and possessed a keen sense of expat personality types.

"I'm really surprised you guys are going back to where you came from," she said. "I expected you to take another posting."

"Why?"

"You just don't seem the type."

"What do you mean? We really like where we come from."

"It's not about that. You travel every chance you get. You love all the adventure of living here. I've seen so many people spend all their time abroad pining for home. They thrive going back. It is really hard for people like you who take advantage of every minute they are living somewhere else to go back where they came from."

"We'll be OK; it's a nice place."

"I'm sorry, but I think you are going to struggle. Talk to each other a lot and be careful."

I knew what she meant. We had thrown ourselves into life in Beijing, never treating it like it was a temporary stop. I wanted to do the same thing when we returned. I have never been a "remember when" guy, and I didn't want to find myself in Maplewood pining for Beijing and muttering about how things were there.

In college, it drove me crazy when people said, "These are the best years of your life." It seemed insane to write off the next six decades and I was no more ready to throw in the towel at forty-one than I had been at twenty-one. I fought the urge to proclaim our stint in China the highlight of our lives or give in to feeling maudlin about leaving.

On my blog I wrote, "Feel free to smack me in a few years if you hear me say, 'Did I ever tell you about the time my band played this big festival in China?'"

But I was far from done with Woodie Alan. After the kids

went to bed, I rushed off to late-night recording sessions at the apartment studio of a French friend of Zhang Yong's who was helping us finish the CD. We also continued to play as many gigs as possible—at our favorite bars, at the U.S. ambassador's residence, at a series of corporate parties, at an American Chamber of Commerce meeting. We had reached a new level of professionalism where these high-paying gigs felt natural. We also had a record deal, with Guitar China, a company that would manufacture and distribute *Beijing Blues*—if we could complete the recording before I left.

When we headed south for a three-city tour that began in Zhang Yong's hometown of Nanjing, his parents invited us over for dinner. Their apartment was in a large complex of identical buildings a half hour outside downtown. It was an impeccably clean two-bedroom, decorated in white. I expected Zhang Yong's father, a retired military college instructor, to be tough and flinty eyed, but he was quiet and friendly, flashing the same kind, bemused smile that I had seen on his son many times.

His mother, a tall, handsome woman, stood in her small kitchen wearing an apron and cooking continuously, putting dish after dish down on the table, talking a mile a minute as she cooked. The food was simple, fresh, and tasty. She surprised me by pouring a nice bottle of cabernet into elegant little crystal glasses.

As she spoke about the pain of having a musician for a child, Zhang Yong ate and smiled, unperturbed by his mother's litany of disappointments. He had clearly heard it all before.

"I encouraged him to be a musician," she said. "But I thought it was a hobby, a great thing to do, but not for a life. I kept waiting for him to grow out of it, get a real job, and settle down, but he just kept riding his bike and playing music!"

Zhang Yong had lived all over China, always finding steady work as a musician before growing restless and moving on, sometimes just leaving a note on the kitchen table for a live-in girlfriend to find in the morning. He still rode his bike to most of our shows, his bass secured on his back, despite living at Beijing's northern edge, about twenty miles from downtown.

A few years earlier, his parents had used much of their savings to buy him an apartment close to theirs. Then they spent more money remodeling it. Zhang Yong thanked them, spent a night in the place, and sold it the next day, using the money to buy a small apartment in Beijing, providing stability as he returned to his itinerant ways.

As she told this story, she came up behind Zhang Yong and playfully smacked his head. He kept eating. His father was sitting in a comfortable recliner a few feet away, laughing. Whatever pain Zhang Yong had caused his parents, they were clearly a loving family.

"We should have had another one!" she exclaimed. Zhang Yong was born before the one-child policy had taken effect, so they could have had more children. "But this one was enough to keep us busy! I tried to keep him in line with regular spankings but nothing worked. He was naughty."

She turned to me. "You people don't believe in hitting your kids, do you? How many do you have?"

"I have three. No, we don't hit them."

"*Ai!* I don't know how you could do that. Impossible!"

"What kind of job do you do?" I asked.

"I'm retired but guess what I did; it used to be the most respected job in China, and now it's the least respected."

She stood before me, hands on her hips. I hesitated and thought, while everyone ate and drank and she looked down at me, waiting for an answer.

"You worked in a factory?"

"Exactly! The foreigner knows! Ha! Very good. Eat some more pork!"

She picked up a tray of sautéed sliced pork and handed it to me, then asked Woodie if he had "a real job." Pleased with his affirmative response, she turned to Lu Wei.

"And you?"

"No. No job. I'm a drummer!"

"Do you own an apartment?"

"No."

"Do you own a car?"

"No."

"Do you have a wife or kids?"

"No."

Lu Wei was smiling, enjoying this parry, and maybe missing his own mom. But Zhang Yong's mother was unsparing.

"You have nothing! You need to grow up. You are not a child anymore."

She was hectoring, but with a smile. She was irresistible, and we were all enjoying this performance. When Woodie and I first got together, I was thrilled to have found such a great musical mate. I never could have guessed that he would end up bringing me so deeply into Chinese life.

The immersion was part of what I enjoyed on our tours. We stayed in simple business-class hotels that cost about $20 a night and were located in solid, quiet middle-class neighborhoods. I woke up hours before my bandmates, strolling the neighborhoods, just watching people go about their lives. In Suzhou, I walked the streets alone for an hour, before stopping in a local noodle shop for a big breakfast bowl of spicy soup noodles. A three-year-old at the next table, with a shaved head except for a rounded patch in front, pointed at me and said, over and over, "*Wei gou ren chi mian!*" (The foreigner eats noodles!) His father shushed him, embarrassed, but I laughed, gave a thumbs-up, and said, "*Hao chi!*" (Tastes great.)

We ended the tour with three shows in two days in the lovely lakeside town of Hangzhou, including appearances at a packed jazz club and at the Asia Pacific Harmonica Festival. We took the stage of a grand two-thousand-seat theater after a tiny old Japanese man in tails playing classical music to prerecorded tracks and before the eighty-member Hong Kong Orchestra played Beethoven under the direction of a flamboyant conductor. Other performers included a pair of stout, lederhosen-wearing Eastern Europeans playing duets of Hungarian folk songs and a young Malaysian group who performed with a fantastic break dance troupe dressed in wild fluorescent outfits.

After our three-song acoustic performance, we ran through the rain to a waiting van, which whisked us across town for the last gig of our tour.

"When you asked me to come jam at the Stone Boat last year, I never could have imagined a year later I'd end up performing at the Asia Pacific Harmonica Festival," Dave said with a laugh. "I'm glad I walked through that door when you opened it."

# CHAPTER 32

# BABY PLEASE DON'T GO

We pushed our move-out date back a week so we could host our fourth and final Thanksgiving in Beijing. Every year we filled our house with a mix of friends, always including at least one group celebrating the holiday for the first time. We had Israeli, Chinese, Austrian, Kenyan, Ethiopian, and Australian guests.

Hosting this event and cooking our own turkey made me feel like an adult more than anything else ever had. No matter how old I got, I still felt like heading for the kids' tables back home at Thanksgiving. But in China, being in charge of the meal, explaining the rituals to our guests, and cooking and carving the bird had made me feel distinctly grown up. We enjoyed one last grand gathering in our Riviera house, raising a toast of Riesling to friendship and to the expat life.

As much as we enjoyed this gathering, it was hard to shake a grandiose, melancholy feeling that we were gathering for our Last Supper. Not everyone was sympathetic to my dramatic sense of impending loss, however. I learned this the next day when I stopped by the Orchard for lunch with owner Lisa Minder, who scoffed at my angst.

"These are rich people's problems," she said dismissively. "Keep some perspective."

It was true that we were trading one privileged existence for another, but I didn't think we should feel guilty about mourning our loss. It was weighing particularly heavily on Becky, who felt responsible for plunging our family into chaos, a feeling reinforced by Anna's daily asking, "Why does Mommy have to move back?"

"I hate ripping you away from here," she said late one night as we lay in bed. "It feels rotten making the kids leave in the middle of the school year and being the Yoko Ono of Woodie Alan—the wife who ends the band."

"That's nonsense." I sat up and turned toward her. "Your job brought us here; your success gave us all this opportunity and now it's taking it away. It's how it had to be.

"And you're not ending Woodie Alan. I don't know how, but we have more life left in us."

"You can come back and play shows," she said hopefully. "It's just a plane ride away."

I laughed at her typical insistence that we could do it all if we just tried hard enough. It was an attitude that could be exhausting but that pushed us far and always helped me feel that anything was possible. I owed a lot to my wife's can-do optimism.

"It's a long plane ride, but maybe I can come back for some festivals or special shows. We'll work it out."

WHEN NIK DEOGUN, the *Wall Street Journal*'s foreign editor, came over for dinner in the midst of a China visit, we told the kids to be on their best behavior. "The guy on his way is Mommy's boss," I explained.

I proudly watched all three children politely shake hands, hold eye contact, and say hello. The boys scattered, but Anna sat down with the adults as we dug into Hou Ayi's dumplings.

She looked Nik in the eye and asked, "Why does my mommy have to move back to America?"

For months we had been answering this question with, "Her boss says she has to." Now the boss was here and Anna wasn't going to let him slip away. When no one answered the question, she asked it again, louder.

"Because people in New Jersey don't know enough about China," Nik said. "And we need you to help us understand this place."

I thought I saw Anna rolling her eyes as she got up and walked away, but maybe I was just projecting.

I PAID VISITS to the doctor, the tailor, the rug store, and the "leather lady," who was making me two coats. I finally took a cooking class with Hou Ayi because I didn't want to return without knowing how to make those great dumplings; she also taught me how to prepare gong bao chicken and spicy tofu. I used to be a pretty good cook and I needed to sharpen those chops again after three and a half years of having most of my meals prepared for me.

Eli was still counting down the days until we moved, seemingly without a second thought about what we were leaving behind. Anna remained somewhat sad and frightened. Jacob was marching bravely forward but also dreading saying good-bye to his extraordinarily close group of friends. He had fully embraced his British education, speaking with a slight accent and saying that he wanted to "attend university at Oxford or Cambridge."

One evening, I leaned against the metal gate in front of our house and watched Jacob and his best friend, Kerk, cross the street. They walked in lockstep, Kerk's left leg moving in sync with Jacob's right. "Waddle!" Jacob yelled, and they both laughed, pointed their toes out and walked on, swaying to the sides like penguins, still perfectly in sync.

Kerk and his Chinese Malaysian family lived directly across the street and the two boys were practically roommates, running back and forth to and from each other's houses. They rode the bus to school together, were in the same class, and spent every possible minute in each other's company, developing their own private language, which required few words to convey a world of meaning. It was beautiful to watch, and my heart ached thinking about the upcoming demise of this day-to-day interaction.

I admired Jacob's stoicism. My family also moved when I was ten—from one end of Pittsburgh's Squirrel Hill neighborhood to the other. I threw fits, cried myself to sleep, and threatened not to honor this one-mile shift away from my gang of friends and into a new school zone. Jacob was much braver. He fully understood what the move would mean for him, but he was not allowing it to ruin his last weeks in Beijing.


WE MET A group of friends for an extended multicourse dinner at Da Dong, one of Beijing's best duck restaurants. We enjoyed a succulent modernized version of our adopted city's signature dish and a great spread of scallops, eggplant, and salty beef. Afterward, we climbed into the back of a cab and began zipping home.

Becky seemed lost in thought before speaking. "I feel like a traitor for leaving," she said. "It's like we are abandoning the team."

I had been having the same thought, though it made no sense. We had arrived in Beijing planning to stay for a defined time and had never seriously considered doing anything else. Yet leaving felt like a form of surrender. We had been to so many farewell parties for others, had so many emotional good-byes, and one of the many mixed emotions these events elicited was a sense of superiority.

The unspoken moral was: "They're abandoning the ship but we are still here, because we're tough. We're real. And now we will bond even more closely with the other robust souls who remain." We are put-down-roots people, loyalists to whatever our cause is, so being on the traitorous side felt deeply wrong. It was wrenching to walk away from the expat life and the community we loved being a part of. Maybe it was ourselves we worried about selling out.

# CHAPTER 33

# TOMORROW NEVER KNOWS

leaning out our kids' playroom one Saturday afternoon offered a reminder of our privileged positions. We filled a dozen bags with toys and clothes for a local orphanage and a few more with items that seemed beneath donating. When I took the third such bag to the garbage can, I found two Riviera maintenance workers sorting through our garbage. They apologized, but I asked how old their children were and ran back in to get them a bag full of appropriate action-hero figures and games. They thanked me and continued to sort for another half an hour, replaced soon after they left by two other guys; I also brought them better toys.

When the movers arrived, we were frantically sorting through one room while they loaded another. Our delay was largely a result of the mad dash to do it all before we left, rather than methodically preparing to leave. Despite my urging that she take a few days off, Becky worked until the end, editing stories and meeting with her staff.

With our house finally emptied, we were right back where we started in Beijing—living out of suitcases in a service apartment.

The relief I felt at being done with the heavy lifting allowed me to temporarily overlook what it really meant: our life in Beijing was rapidly coming to an end. The difficulty of the move over-rode the emotion; we were just happy to be done with it.

All that suppressed emotion was bound to bubble up, but it still caught us by surprise. On the last day of school, the Dul-wich school honored its twenty departing students at an as-sembly, calling each one up and presenting a signed picture of the entire student body. As Eli and Jacob stood in front looking a bit bewildered, Becky started sobbing, her bottled-up regret and sorrow pouring out in a torrent. She was hugging our Aus-tralian friend Karen, also about to depart and also struggling to hold herself together. The two of them were holding each other as if they would drown if they let go.

Often worried about how leaving would impact the kids and me, Becky had neglected her own sense of loss, but she too had made irreplaceable friendships and bonds in China. When I reached over and grabbed her hand, she squeezed hard and buried her face in the crook of my neck. I kissed the top of her head and smoothed her hair. I looked up and saw Eli staring at us. Already dazed, he now appeared astonished and a little scared by what he saw.

When the assembly ended, I jumped up to reassure Eli and take pictures of the boys and their friends, several of whom were crying. Jacob and another departing classmate stood in the middle looking bewildered. The emotions were becoming too much to bear.

Even Eli was starting to crack. The night before, he cried himself to sleep, breaking his sobs for a moment to ask when we could return to Beijing for a visit. I was happy that he was dealing with the complexity and mixed emotions; the rest of us had been processing this loss for months.

The next morning, I said good-bye to Ding Ayi, who had worked for us from day one and had a lovely, meaningful relationship with Anna. She had been a big part of our family and now she was sobbing as I handed her an envelope full of severance cash and wished her well. I wanted to hug her but it just wasn't appropriate.

WE PLAYED FOUR gigs in my last eight days in Beijing, which put off my inevitable good-byes with my bandmates as long as possible. During a break at one of the shows, a corporate party for the *Wall Street Journal*'s Chinese-language website, we sat at a table in a swank Japanese restaurant, with Lu Wei talking animatedly to Woodie while I ate tuna sashimi. I could only understand parts of his rant.

"Lu Wei said he can't believe that after we all worked so hard on the CD, we won't even get to celebrate with a release show," Woodie explained.

"Tell him I will come back." I was speaking impulsively, thinking of Becky's suggestion that I return for shows. "We *will* have a CD release concert!"

We had an ongoing series of good-bye gatherings—kids' parties; an official transition affair for the paper, with sources, dignitaries, and government officials; an evening to meet readers of my Chinese-language column; and a farewell party for our friends at the Orchard. With time running short, Woodie Alan's final performance was on the same night as Becky's office dinner at a dumpling restaurant. This ended up creating a happy synchronicity, combining all our different crowds into one true farewell, as virtually the entire *WSJ* China staff descended on our gig, in a new basement space being run by a friend's bar, with a sprawling, vintage rathskeller feel.

I kept my emotions in check, trying to just focus on the music and savor every moment. At the end of our first set, we launched into "You're Gonna Make Me Lonesome When You Go," the song I had used to bid so many friends farewell. The lyrics caught in my throat before coming out in an impassioned wail.

*You're gonna make me wonder what I'm doing /
leaving you so far behind. . . . / You're gonna make
me give myself a good talking to . . . You're gonna
make me lonesome when you go.*

I was singing these words, altered to fit my situation, to my friends, to my bandmates, to my day-to-day life, and to China itself.

We closed with "Soulshine," with Woodie, Zhang Yong, and I singing the final line in three-part harmony, stretching the last note out as long as we could, before it finally tailed off. The crowd exploded, but I heard only the silence of the band.

Everyone hung out for a while, chatting and taking pictures, but eventually I had to say good-bye to my bandmates. We embraced in small hugs, with me promising that I would return for a CD release show. Lu Wei and Zhang Yong left with their friends, then I helped Woodie carry his gear to his car. He was struggling through a tough family time, which made leaving him and the band all the more difficult.

"Hang in there," I said. "E-mail or call me any time. I know this is a hard time for you and I . . ."

"I know," he said. "I know."

We didn't try to recapture our entire history. There was nothing left to say; we both understood how much our partnership had meant and would continue to mean to each of us. We were brothers.

We shook hands and hugged lightly out on the street, then he climbed into his white compact car and I watched him turn around and drive away, with a final wave.

TWO DAYS LATER, at 6:30 a.m., we dragged ourselves out into the frigid, dark December morning. We needed two cars to haul all our bags to the airport, so Mr. Dou and Mr. Lu were both there. They went upstairs to lug suitcases down. With everything in the car, I returned and picked up Anna, half asleep and wrapped in a blanket. When I came back down, our friend Ellen Carberry was standing in the lobby hugging Becky. She had run over from a nearby compound to say good-bye, one final teary farewell.

I joined my family in Mr. Dou's car—we had filled Lu's vehicle with bags so we could all be together. I sat in the front seat and reached my arm back to grab Becky's hand. Jacob, sitting behind me, with his head pressed against the window, reached up and looped his arm over mine, squeezing tight.

We were all silent as we pulled out into the slowly brightening morning, everyone looking out the windows and saying our own internal good-byes to Beijing Riviera. The place that had seemed so exotic when we arrived now felt very much like home.

Three years ago, when Mr. Dou picked us up, we handed him a camera and asked him to take a picture of us, looking bedraggled in front of our teeming baggage cart. Now, standing in the same airport, we handed the camera to someone else and asked him to snap a family photo with Mr. Dou, who had been by our side through so much.

As we took off, I leaned over Jacob's shoulder, holding his hand as we both looked silently out the window, watching

China fade away. I turned my head and looked at Becky, sitting directly behind me with the other children. We locked eyes and had a conversation without saying a word. I snaked my arm back through the seats and we took each other's hands and squeezed hard.

I was very happy that we weren't heading directly back to New Jersey. Figuring that we would need time to acclimate and knowing that our belongings wouldn't arrive for two months anyhow, we scheduled a week in Hawaii and a few days visiting the Camerons, who had relocated to San Diego. This wasn't as grandiose of a vacation as it sounds—more like time in a decompression chamber. When it was finally time for the final leg of our trip, we were ready to head back and start reestablishing Maplewood as our home.

The five-hour cross-country flight felt short. California, which once seemed too far to live, now felt like a suburb of New York. When we were finally descending into Newark, Jacob looked out at the ground growing closer by the second.

"There it is, Dad," he said. "New Jersey. Our adventure's over."

I was momentarily staggered by my ten-year-old son's pithy ability to get to the heart of the matter. But I couldn't let his comment stand unchallenged. It sounded too much like admitting defeat.

"No, Jacob," I said. "Our Chinese adventure is over. A new adventure is just beginning."

# I SHALL RETURN

By the time we landed in Maplewood, I had a hard drive full of music tracks e-mailed from Woodie, who was working with the producer to finish mixing our album. Throwing myself back into Woodie Alan even as my family went through the process of reestablishing our lives in New Jersey served as a daily reminder of all I had accomplished in China.

Just as when we moved to Beijing, I was astounded by the ease with which the kids were able to transition into new schools and make new friends. They were also rekindling some dimmed connections. Jacob had attended kindergarten and first grade in Maplewood and was returning in the middle of fifth grade. Eli and Anna had never been in the school system.

I felt a pit in my stomach leaving my sons in the principal's office with anxious eyes on their first day of school, but they emerged smiling seven hours later. They felt like celebrities, hailed as kids who arrived in the middle of the year from China.

We waded through the sixty-four boxes delivered from storage and enjoyed suburban life free of language misunderstandings and tense drives—for about a month. That was the length of our regular return visits and when it passed, we all deflated as the simple reality that we weren't going anywhere settled in.

Anna told me daily that she liked her Chinese school better and asked when we could return. Jacob talked about his Beijing buddies and fell apart when he lost his Dulwich College ski hat, which represented his previous life. Even Eli, who had spent eighteen months in Beijing asking to return to America, cried himself to sleep, saying, "When I said I hated China, I really just missed the United States. But now . . ."

Now he missed Beijing.

I carried a deep sense of loss I never really felt while living in China and thinking about my American home. Then, I longed for specific people or places, sometimes profoundly, but I never felt truly desperate, because I knew that someday I would return. My Beijing life, on the other hand, was truly gone, a glittering memory in the rearview mirror destined to grow fainter every day.

Things felt better after our shipment from Beijing arrived six weeks later. The three hundred boxes delivered on a snowy day prompted my aunt Joan to say, "I hope that no one is going to China hoping to shop, because there can't be anything left."

It might have been overkill, but the altar tables, vases, Buddha heads, Miao silver artwork, and terracotta warriors were a great comfort to us. It felt good to see these reminders of China in our New Jersey home, melding our two lives together. We attempted to turn this fusion into our regular existence.

I got back in touch with Tom Davis, who was settling into life in his hometown of Butte, Montana, and raising his two girls as a single dad. We made plans to meet in Pittsburgh for a Steelers game, and I marveled at pictures of his youngest daughter, Sudha, playing softball and zipping around the bases on her prosthetic legs, with snow-capped mountains rising on the horizon. I realized my friend and his family were going to be just fine.

Music kept me moving forward, even as it anchored me to my past. The editors at *Guitar World* brought me back into the fold; I continued to work on the *Beijing Blues* CD; and my friend Dave Gomberg, a frequent jamming partner from pre-China days, invited me to perform with his Maplewood band. We took the stage in front of one hundred neighbors and nailed "Beijing Blues." It felt easy and automatic, helping me realize that I could stand on my own as a musician, without Woodie Alan—and so could the songs I had written for the band.

Dave was amazed by my transformation. "You left for China as a guy who plays guitar and came back a musician," he said.

But singing "Beijing Blues" so far from Beijing made me long for my band and our regular performances with a ferocity that startled me and that I really couldn't share with anyone. I didn't want to burden Rebecca or make her feel guilty for returning early, and few others could really understand. To paraphrase Neil Young, I hit the city and I lost my band, and I often felt lost without it.

I threw myself into finishing up our album from afar, choosing mixes, approving artwork, and writing liner notes. When I interviewed ZZ Top's bearded wonder Billy Gibbons and told him about Woodie Alan, he was fascinated. He asked to hear some tracks, then e-mailed back,

This is the best Chinese blues I've ever heard. Who knew?

I stopped the presses to add this quote to the back of the CD. I was ready to return to China for the album release shows but held off buying my ticket because I had not heard back from Yechen, my Mandarin teacher-turned-monk. I had e-mailed him several months earlier saying that I was returning and wanted to see him. I remained haunted by how lost he seemed to be the last time I saw him, on Huashan, and by my failure to offer him more honest advice when he was weighing a return to London versus entering a monastery. I meant it when I said that I would try to come back to the mountain, and I wanted to honor my pledge.

I contemplated the trip at a Grateful Dead concert, watching my old friend, guitarist Warren Haynes, rip it up with a new band. Then my phone vibrated, signaling a new e-mail had arrived. I glanced down and saw the familiar Chinese characters for Yechen's name. His message was short and simple:

Leaving mountain to start my life. Like to see you.

I booked a two-week trip to China, reserving two days in the middle to see Yechen wherever he turned up.


LANDING IN BEIJING less than six months after we left felt completely natural. I walked out of customs, saw Mr. Lu, our old reliable taxi driver, waiting for me and felt like I had never really left. But as we pulled onto the highway and I gave him directions to my friend's house in a compound near Riviera, I was overcome by a simple contradiction: though I felt like I was coming home, I no longer had a home there.

Monochromatic Beijing—grayish brown and covered with dust—suddenly looked rather bizarre; it made Maplewood seem like a tropical rain forest. We turned onto the road that runs behind the Riviera and I momentarily thought that Mr. Lu had gotten lost. The street was unrecognizable. The tall trees that lined it had been removed to make way for the massive construction of a new subway line that now dominated the formerly sleepy lane and had completely transformed the neighborhood. I had been gone less than six months, but it might as well have been six years.

Construction was also under way up and down the nearby Jing Shun Lu, with long stretches of buildings—and even entire villages—torn down to make way for the subway. The Sunhe Kite Market I had frequented so many times stood alone, surrounded by rubble; it too would be gone in a few months. The whole area was unrecognizable from the time we arrived in Beijing four years earlier.

I dropped my bags and my guitar at my friends' house, jumped on a bike, and pedaled over to the Riv. I turned into our old circle, and the *ayi* sweeping the street with a twig broom lit up when she saw me. "*Ni hao!*" she shouted. "*Anna zai nar?*" (Hi. Where's Anna?)

I braced for a flood of strong emotions before visiting our old house, but it never came. I shouldn't have been surprised, as this mirrored my experience returning to Maplewood for the first time, when seeing our house occupied by tenants turned out to be an anticlimactic nonevent. Home is where my family is; the building where we live is just there to contain us. But seeing the house did make me miss Becky and the kids ferociously; being here without them made me feel off-kilter.

I felt untethered, floating through other people's lives without the anchor of my family. There was only one place where Beijing felt unambiguously like home—on the bandstand with Woodie Alan. When I was performing, I had no ambivalence about where I should be.

I was nervous driving to our sole rehearsal, worried about whether or not it would be enough before playing ten shows in ten days. I pulled into the parking lot of a dingy strip mall on the tattered, southern fringes of Beijing and was met by a heavily tattooed, peroxide-blond Chinese guy, whose face was obscured by massive white sunglasses. He grabbed my guitar and motioned for me to follow him into the tattoo parlor/music studio he managed. We entered a small shop, where a young Chinese woman sat in a chair getting tattooed by another employee, and he led the way down a steep pair of steps. Inside a basement practice space I found Lu Wei, Zhang Yong, and Woodie behind their instruments.

We exchanged happy but brief greetings as the blond guy plugged me in. Without calling out a song, I simply started strumming the chords to Bob Dylan's "Meet Me in the Morning." Everyone fell in behind me and all my worries vanished. It felt like we had played the day before. I heard my singing and playing elevate and knew that the sum of us together was greater than the parts; in my case, far greater. Musical chemistry had once again topped verbal communication.

We rehearsed for two hours, went out for a great, festive dinner, and then played our first show, at one of our favorite spots, the Stone Boat, which was once again featuring live music. We played five shows in the next three days, steadily getting better. A day later, the rest of the band departed for Shenzhen in southern China where I would meet them for three gigs. First, I would visit Yechen in his hometown of Wuxi, near Shanghai.

I felt a surprising surge of emotion in the airport terminal, which had been the launching pad for so many memorable trips. Walking by the Häagen-Dazs stand near the security line reminded me of my kids clamoring for ice cream every time we were rushing to catch a flight. A big part of me wished that I was boarding a plane to New Jersey instead of venturing deeper into China on my own, but I was also excited to see Yechen after months of wondering how he was doing.

He was waiting when I walked out of security, looking much healthier than he had a year earlier. His long hair was pulled back in a ponytail, and he was wearing a black polo-style shirt and long khaki shorts. He was with an attractive young woman, whom he introduced as his cousin Karen, our driver for the day.

We drove to a lakeside teahouse and chatted easily for hours. Yechen had always seemed to be a lone wolf, with no connections to anything or anyone except his mother, but I quickly realized that there was a long line of people who had also been drawn in by his quiet magnetism.

Yechen was the oldest of four cousins, Karen explained, and they all looked up to him as a sage older brother. Just two days earlier, they had learned that he had spent two years on the mountain—everyone thought he was in Beijing, which his parents still believed. The cousins were shocked but not surprised.

"He always had his own ideas," Karen explained. Before moving to London, she said, he taught Chinese at a Wuxi middle school, where he was renowned for having students who delivered the highest test scores, despite the lowest workloads. He dyed his hair blond, convincing school officials this was because of a medical condition. Also, Karen said, "He was a real fashion guy" who would only wear clothes bought in Shanghai.

That night we had dinner with two university friends who had lost touch with Yechen for over ten years but found his cell number thanks to the work of another former classmate, who was now a police officer. They simply had to find out what had become of their smart, funny, insightful friend. I asked the ladies what they thought Yechen would become during their time in college, and they answered in unison, "*Laoshi*" (teacher). This reinforced my belief that he had found his calling long before he went searching.

As we all filed out of the restaurant, Yechen turned to me. "They want to go sing karaoke," he said. "You don't want to go do that, do you?"

Actually, I did. I had spent three and a half years in this karaoke-crazed nation without ever partaking. Yechen honored my request, and his reticence vanished inside the singing room. He took over the computer controls, adding flashing lights and seeking English songs for me to sing. I tackled "Copacabana," but sadly no one understood how funny it was and politely applauded my awful rendition.

Yechen was engrossed, singing Chinese pop duets with his friends in a beautiful, clearly enunciated tenor voice. "I think he's still the fashion guy inside," Karen whispered in my ear.

I was happy to see him having so much fun and when I was ready to leave, I told him I could make my way back to the hotel, but he insisted on having Karen drive me. He walked me to the lobby, where we hugged and I told him to stay in touch.

Early the next morning I flew off to Shenzhen to meet up with the band. On the plane, I laughed at the incongruity of leaving Yechen in a karaoke room, belting out Taiwanese pop. Later, as I walked through bustling, sweltering Shenzhen, I received a text message from Yechen: I am always a monk, although I am not stay temple or mountain.

I wrote him back: I know that. It is inside you. You can live in both worlds. Don't feel guilty for enjoying it.

I thought that the root of his problem was that he was tormented by the very thing that I was celebrated for—an ability to live in more than one world. I viewed it as a great strength, while he seemed to consider it a debilitating weakness, with a constant need to choose sides.

WE PLAYED THREE crazy gigs in two days in Shenzhen, one night being ferried between clubs by a bus supplied by the owners, and the next night performing in a suburban outpost with girls dancing on the tables between bands. Afterward, we sat at a table at an outdoor restaurant at 3:00 a.m., watching a vibrant street life, with workers hosing down the sidewalk and others stopping for meals on their way home from long days on the job. We ate a whole fish prepared Sichuan style, served in a large metal pan and covered with fiery little peppers; tiny, numbing peppercorns; cloves of garlic; and slices of ginger. We toasted with tiny plastic cups of warm beer before heading back to our decrepit hotel and its hole-ridden sheets. I wondered how I could ever explain why I missed China so much.

Back in Beijing, we played two more shows and I visited more friends. On my last day, Woodie Alan got together for a morning acoustic jam session on the beautiful park grounds of the Temple of Heaven, one of Beijing's most famous historical sites. We joined the many elderly people who gathered there on weekends to sing and play traditional Chinese music and were happily welcomed by a curious crowd who gathered around and seemed to enjoy the music.

Afterward, we went to a nearby hot pot restaurant for lunch, dunking thin-sliced lamb and beef, tofu, vegetables, and noodles into seasoned broth then dipping them into sesame sauce. As we ate, we talked about how much we had enjoyed this reunion.

In the five months I'd been gone, Woodie Alan had continued playing, adding another American, a far more technically accomplished guitarist than me. I had mixed feelings about this replacement; it felt like an act of adultery, but the ease with which the five of us slipped back together made me happy that the band had pressed on. Woodie had not invited the other guitarist to any of these shows, despite my repeated urgings. Now the band's current lineup was also in danger, because saxophonist Dave Loevinger would also be returning to the United States soon. Woodie said he just couldn't continue the band.

"Playing all these shows with you made me realize that the band has just not been right without you, even though we've been good," he said. "I can't play music I don't love and feel from the inside anymore. We're going to have to try something different."

I took this as a compliment and an affirmation of my own feelings, but also as a blow. I didn't want to see our band die, but it was no longer up to me. What I really wanted to do was get the group over to the United States. Doing so would close the circle for me. I wanted to show Woodie, Lu Wei, and Zhang Yong around my home country, and I wanted American people to see us together; I believed in the power of music to bridge divides.

I was ready to head back now, though with deeply conflicted feelings. I knew that returning to New Jersey would feel even more like coming home than landing in Beijing ten days earlier had. I had reconnected with many people and reaffirmed most of my thoughts and feelings about my life in Beijing. Now I wanted to get back to my family.

I had accepted that life in China, for Woodie and the rest of the band, and for Yechen, too, had moved on without me. But walking away from the band for a second time, after confirming what a special bond we had, was excruciating. It felt like breaking up with a true love over logistics.

I would have plenty of time to sort it all out—but not here. My clock was now ticking on the other side of the world, in a leafy New Jersey suburb.

# ACKNOWLEDGMENTS

Thank you to Becky, Jacob, Eli, and Anna for the never-ending sense of adventure that made being in China together so much fun. A special eternal thank you to Becky for a lifetime of gently pushing for more.

Thank you to my brother Woodie Wu and my other Woodie Alan soul mates: Dave Loevinger, Lu Wei, and Zhang Yong. I would walk on any stage in the world with you behind me.

Lisa Minder and the Orchard provided Woodie Alan with our first gig and a steady, comfortable home base. Thanks also to Tianxiao and Jianghu Jiuba, Jonathan Ansfield and the Stone Boat, George Smith and Frank's Place.

From the moment I landed in China, I was helped by the kindness of others. Kathy Chen provided expert guidance then and gave this book an insightful read now. Theo Yardley was an endless source of information and inspiration. My Chinese teacher Yechen taught me a tremendous amount about China and much more. Tom Davis was a true friend.

Thank you to Almar Latour, Elana Beiser, Bill Grueskin, Jason Fry, and everyone else at WSJ.com who gave The Expat Life a chance and consistently helped make it better. An active, intelligent readership was also a consistent source of ideas and inspiration.

Thank you to the entire *WSJ* Beijing bureau, especially

Andrew Browne, Jason Dean, Shai Oster, Mei Fong, Loretta Chao, Lily Song, Ellen Zhu, Cui Rong, Sue Feng, and Mr. Dou Changlou, who steered us through Beijing's traffic, both literal and metaphoric. Kersten Zhang's invaluable assistance extended to this book.

The world would be a much more fun place if everyone had friends like our Beijing crew. Many people helped make every day memorable, including: Scott Kronick and Lisa Wei, who have continued to provide us with a second home, Wyatt and Jacqui Cameron, Jim and Theo Yardley, Vivian Nazari and John Scales, Matt and Ellen Carberry, Nathan and Kristi Belete, Dave and Katherine Loevinger, Anna and Chris Holdsworth, Will and Cheryl Latta, Karen and Michael Shagrin, Patrick and Jenn Sullivan, Michael and Lisa Pos, Tony and Georgie Ohlsson, Eric Rosenblum and Titi Liu, Malcolm Lee and Nancy Choy, and Deirdre Smyth and Luc van Son. Maya Alexandri and the Kehillat Beijing family made it fun to be a Fu Man Jew. Vicky, Sean, and the hockey crew helped me do something even more ludicrous than becoming a Chinese rock star.

Thank you, Jim McGregor and Jim Yardley for consistently encouraging me to write this book. Rodger Citron, Jill Drew, Ian Johnson, Diana Kapp, and Danny Rosen provided insightful feedback on early chapters.

Thank you to Echo, Ding Ayi, and Hou Ayi, whose expert childcare freed me up to run around with the band and who were all friendly, stabilizing presences for our frenetic family; to drivers Mr. and Mrs. Lu; to Raymond Wu, Beijing's best tour guide; and to Lao Wang, a brilliant doctor and a gentle soul. Jim Spear and the Schoolhouse provided a great place to write and think. He Li Ying (Linda) was a wonderful teacher, friend, and guide to China.

Thank you to my editor, Hollis Heimbouch, for believing in this book, sharing a vision from our first meeting, and consistently making *Big in China* better. Roe D'Angelo at WSJ Books believed in this idea and helped see it through. Katherine Beitner helped publicize it like the old friend she is. Thank you Lisa Dallos and Michael Wolfson.

With thanks to my parents, Dixie and Suzi, for always providing love, giving me space, and allowing me to dream big.

Thank you, Joan and Ben Cohen for welcoming our family, piles of luggage and all, during visits home and, most recently, for six months while our home was gutted and I wrote this book; and to Carrie and Dave Wells for their support.

My extended family has provided a safety net as I have climbed out onto life's limbs and a grounding that guaranteed I would never get too big for my britches. Thank you all, especially David Paul and Kathy Klein; Laura and Jon Kessler; Hal, Ruth, Molly, Sara, Jenny, and Beth Blumenstein.

David Kann showed me what it takes to be the Bull Goose Looney. Art Rummler, Per Hoffman, Norman Bradford, and Evan Michaelson have shared music and more for many years. Craig Winkelman and Jane Beck urged me to start a blog. Carol Hymowitz encouraged me to write a column.

Thank you to Greg Benson for his sage counsel, Dave Gomberg for the tunes, Jocelyne Cordova for the push to China, and all our Maplewood friends who kept us in their hearts and minds for three-and-a-half years and welcomed us back with open arms.

Thank you to Brad Tolinski, Jeff Kitts, Andy Aledort, Jimmy Brown, and *Guitar World*; Ben Osborne, Susan Price, Lang Whitaker, Dennis Page, and *Slam*; Joe Gesue, Dave Gabel, Tom Matthews, and NBC.com; Kirk West, Bert Holman, and the Allman Brothers Band; and the countless musicians who have soothed my soul, lifted my spirits, and cleared my head. Thank you, Billy Gibbons, Warren Haynes, Derek Trucks, Bruce Iglauer, Joe Bonamassa, Charlie Musselwhite, Col. Bruce Hampton, and Gregg Allman for supporting my music and this book.

I wrote large parts of *Big in China* at the Maplewood, South Orange, and Millburn public libraries. My time there helped me gain a renewed appreciation for just how important libraries are.

RIP: Cathy Davis and Tim "Tragocaster" Lamb.

In loving memory of my grandparents, Anne and Rudy Oppenheimer, and Sarah and M. A. Paul.